DID EVE REALLY HAVE AN EXTRA RIB?

AND OTHER TOUGH QUESTIONS ABOUT THE BIBLE

by
KEN HAM

D0068589

Master Books

First printing: May 2002
Second printing: January 2003

ISBN: 0-89051-370-8
Library of Congress Card Number: 2001098884

Printed in the United States of America

For information regarding author interviews, please contact the publicity department at (870) 438-5288.

Please visit our website for other great titles:
www.masterbooks.net

Table of Contents

Note: The question of whether Eve had an extra rib
is answered on page 51.

BIBLICAL AUTHORITY

BOOK OF GENESIS

History of Man

FOSSIL FACTS

EVOLUTION AND THE DINOSAURS

CREATION EVIDENCE IN SPACE

CREATION VS. EVOLUTION

Evolution's Agenda

Evolution in Education

EVOLUTIONARY INFILTRATION IN THE CHURCH

Biblical

Authority

Q. *The Bible teaches that the earth is only thousands of years old. If people believe in billions of years, can they still be Christians?*

A. On a live radio talk show, a man called up and said, "I object to the way you say that people HAVE to believe in a young earth to be a Christian." I immediately replied, "Sir, I've never said that. If people are born again as the Bible defines, no matter what they believe about the age of the earth, they're saved."

This man then went on and said, "Well do you recognize that it doesn't matter what you believe about the earth's age?"

I then stated, "Now wait a minute, sir. I didn't say that. You see, ultimately, it does matter what you believe about the age of the earth. One of the reasons is that as soon as you allow for billions of years, you've also allowed death, suffering, bloodshed, and disease BEFORE sin. The Bible teaches that death is the penalty for sin. It's the foundation of the gospel."

I went on to explain to him that if you're a Christian and believe in an old earth, that won't stop you from getting to heaven. But it WILL stop you from correctly explaining the gospel message to someone.

Q. *As I read the Bible, I certainly don't get the idea that the Jews believed in evolution — is that correct?*

A. You're right about that. You see, when Peter spoke to the Jews on the Day of Pentecost, he was preaching to a culture that believed in God — they believed in creation. They had the law of Moses and understood about sin. It was a creation-based culture. Therefore, Peter didn't have to convince them about creation or that they were sinners. He had to help them understand that Jesus Christ was the Messiah.

But when Paul preached to the Greeks, he was speaking to a TOTALLY different sort of culture. They had no concept of the God the Jews understood. In fact, the Greeks believed in a form of evolution. They didn't believe in God as Creator, and had no concept of the meaning of sin. As an evolution-based culture, Paul had to first teach them about the true Creator God and an understanding of sin BEFORE they could understand the gospel.

In our Western world, as students come through an education system devoid of the knowledge of God, they're more like Greeks than Jews, and that's how we need to approach them if we're going to be truly successful in evangelism.

Q. *The Bible tells us that "without faith it is impossible" to please God. What sort of faith is this? Surely it doesn't mean that Christians should just BLINDLY believe God's Word.*

A. The exciting thing about being a Christian is that it's not blind faith. In fact, it's the evolutionist who has the blind faith.

Sadly, I've found many Christians who don't see this. I've often found that when I've asked Christian young people how they know God is Creator, usually one of them will tell me that they have to have blind faith.

But I explain to them that we're commanded by Peter to give reasons for what we believe. We're also told in Scripture that the evidence that God is Creator is so great, if anyone doesn't believe, they're without excuse (Rom. 1:20). I then teach these youngsters how to defend their faith logically; that design means a designer. The information in our highly complex genes couldn't arise by chance — an intelligence had to be responsible. The evidence fits with the Bible, not with "chance" evolution!

What kind of faith is the Christian faith? It's a logical, defensible faith, right from the very first verse.

Q. *We constantly hear people say that the Bible is only a religious book, not a science book. Is that true?*

A. Actually the Bible teaches us many things, including science. For example, in order to do any science at all, you must be able to start with energy, matter, and time.

Evolution assumes that time was already in existence. Then it makes the assumption that there was a sufficient amount of energy and matter within that time that caused the big bang. What evolution can't explain is where that time, energy, and matter came from. They have to have it already there.

Well, Genesis 1:1 tells us, *"In the beginning God created the heaven and the earth."*

The Bible is the ONLY religious book that starts with a scientific statement and explains the origin of everything that we know to exist. The rest of Genesis 1 goes on to list the rest of the acts of creation and many of the physical laws that we use in science. Therefore, the Bible is not only a religious book, but it's also a book of science!

Q: *A Christian told me recently that the days of creation can't be ordinary days because the Bible says that "a day is like a thousand years." Did he have a valid point?*

A. I feel like tearing my hair out every time I hear this argument. The passage that likens a day to a thousand years is found in 2 Peter 3. In this passage, Peter is explaining that God is OUTSIDE of time. So the context of this chapter has nothing to do with the days of creation.

That's not all. You can't use a passage from the New Testament, which was written in Greek, to determine the meaning of a word in Genesis written in Hebrew! The meaning of the word depends upon its context according to the rules of that language!

Besides, if people were consistent, then they should reinterpret the day everywhere else it's used in the Old Testament. Why not say that Jonah was in the whale three thousand years instead of three days! Of course, that would make nonsense of the text.

No, the word "day" in the context of the language of Genesis 1 has to mean an ordinary day!

Q. *What logical answer can Christians give to that difficult question "How do we know there's a God?"*

A. When I ask that question in the typical church, the usual answer is that we should just accept by faith that God has always existed. Even though that's true, God's Word commands us to give reasons for what we believe. Otherwise, non-Christians may think Christianity is blind faith, but it's not.

When I'm asked this question, I first of all use examples like the presidents' sculpted heads on Mt. Rushmore. I explain that they didn't get there by millions of years of wind and water erosion. It's obvious someone using intelligence carved them. Now consider our brain. It's far more complicated than the most advanced computer. Just as someone designed and constructed the computer, obviously a greater intelligence designed and constructed our brain.

Actually, nowhere in the world do we ever see information systems like machines coming from disorder by chance. It always takes intelligence, which means information. This means you have to have information to start with. Thus, the only logical way to think is that you must start with infinite information — an infinite intelligence! The answer's in Genesis — "In the beginning, God."

Q. *If Genesis was just a metaphor or symbolic, wouldn't that mean ALL Christian doctrine, including the gospel, was based on a myth?*

A. You're quite right. If Genesis was just a metaphor, we'd have to throw out all Christian doctrine, and the gospel itself would be meaningless.

Over the years, I've had a number of pastors insist that Genesis 1–11 was just a metaphor — that it wasn't meant to be taken as literal history.

I like to challenge these Christian leaders by referring them to the genealogies that are repeated in the Old and New Testaments. For instance, in Luke the genealogy is listed to show that Jesus Christ became a descendant of Adam. As you read through the genealogy, it mentions a particular person being a descendant of a specific person and so on all the way back to — a metaphor?

Of course not — these genealogies go all the way back through real people to a real first man, Adam — otherwise they'd be meaningless.

Paul, in Corinthians, compares the first Adam and the last Adam (Jesus Christ) to explain the origin of sin and death and the need for a Savior. If the first Adam was just a metaphor, then this makes the whole message of the gospel meaningless.

Q. *Surely you wouldn't say the Bible was a man-made work, would you?*

A. We're told in God's Word that people, moved by God's spirit, wrote down the words of the Bible exactly as God wanted them written. As we're told in the Book of Timothy, ALL Scripture is inspired by God.

Because the Bible is infallible, we can trust every word. It's not the word of men, but actually the word of God. If it were man's word, then it wouldn't be infallible.

I received a letter from a pastor objecting to the stand we take on the six literal days of creation. He insisted that we can't take the Bible literally because, after all, it's only a human work. This same pastor accepts the millions of years of evolution.

Think of how inconsistent this pastor is. He says that the Bible is only a human work; therefore you don't have to take it literally. But with evolution, which is a human work, he DOES take it literally and doesn't question it. This is typical of many Christian leaders today.

Oh, how the Church today needs to proclaim with the Psalmist that "Thy Word is true from the beginning." Let's get back to the authority of the Book of Genesis and ALL of God's *infallible* Word.

Q: *Surely all Christians would say it's vital to believe in original sin and in Adam's fall, wouldn't they?*

A. Well, I've actually had a number of Christians tell me that the Book of Genesis is NOT essential to the gospel. They say that as long as people believe in Jesus Christ and what He did on the Cross — that's all that's really essential to the gospel!

Imagine a Christian whose church teaches that Genesis is not essential. As long as we tell people about Jesus, that's all that's important. Imagine the following conversation as that person tries to witness to a skeptic.

"Sir, you must believe in Jesus."

"Who is He?" replies the skeptic.

"Well," states the Christian, "He died for your sins."

"Why'd he do that — and what is sin?" the skeptic questions.

The Christian then blurts, "There's a story in Genesis about Adam and Eve and sin — but it's probably just a myth. Don't worry about that — just trust in Jesus."

Could you imagine the skeptic saying, "Wow — what a powerful message!" Not at all!

You see, the history of Genesis and original sin is ABSOLUTELY foundational and essential to understanding the gospel.

Q. *Don't we have to read the New Testament to find out about the gospel of Jesus Christ?*

A. In our children's book, *A is for Adam*, we have a picture of Adam and Eve in the Garden of Eden clothed in lamb's wool. Beside them is a slain lamb.

This drawing is based on the passage in Genesis where we're told that because of sin, God made coats of skins and clothed Adam and Eve. God killed an animal to provide the first blood sacrifice because of sin.

This is a picture of what was to come in Jesus Christ, "the Lamb of God which taketh away the sin of the world." Because of sin, death entered the world.

The only way for man to come back to God was for a perfect man to suffer death and pay the penalty for sin. God sent His only Son to become a man so that He could die and be raised from the dead. In that way, those who trust in Him will be saved for eternity.

The shedding of blood and the clothing of Adam and Eve is a picture of the gospel. If Christians don't believe Genesis is literal history, then the gospel is not to be taken literally either.

Q. *I recently saw a bumper sticker that declared on one side, "The earth does not belong to us." On the other side it stated, "We belong to the earth." Now, that's a popular philosophy of many of the extreme environmentalists. So, the earth belongs to whom?*

A. God tells us that He created the heavens, the earth, and all that is in them. We're also told that He created all things for His pleasure. In other words, according to the Bible, the bumper sticker is right in its first statement — the earth doesn't belong to us. But the person who wrote this sticker fails to realize that our world does belong to God.

Also, in Genesis we're told that God made man from the dust of the earth, but he was made in God's image. God breathed into man, who then became a living soul. So the bumper sticker is wrong. We don't belong to the earth — we belong to God.

Because we're His, God showed His love for us by paying the ultimate price for our sin so we could live forever with Him — He sacrificed His Son on the Cross. Each one of us needs to accept this free gift from the One who owns us and has the TRUE answer to the meaning of life!

Q. *Does the Bible tell us when Satan fell?*

A. Actually, the Bible doesn't say exactly when Satan rebelled against God. In fact, the Bible doesn't even tell us exactly when Satan was created.

The great theologian John Calvin said that the Bible is not about angels, but about man and his relationship with his Creator. Therefore, he says, we're not told a lot about angels.

But I believe there are some things we can glean from Scripture concerning this. In Colossians 1, we're told that Jesus Christ created all things, including all principalities and powers. This must mean that Christ created the angels, including Lucifer. We're not told when, but we could guess that perhaps it was on the first day of creation.

Now at the end of the sixth day of creation, God pronounced everything He'd made as "very good." Now this must have included the angels that He also created. Thus, at the end of the sixth day, even Lucifer must have been "very good." Then God blessed the seventh day.

From all of this, I believe Satan's fall had to be AFTER the creation week — not before.

Q. *Why do we believe in right and wrong and good and bad in the first place?*

A. I had the opportunity recently to interact with a public school teacher.

We debated the creation/evolution issue. At one stage, I asked the teacher whether he taught his students morals — that some things were right and some wrong. He said he did. I then asked him where he obtained these morals.

He smiled and said, "Well I have to be honest and say that they come from the Judeo-Christian ethic and the Bible that our society is based on."

He then told me that because of evolution, it was obvious the Bible wasn't true anyway. I then asked him if he taught his children these same morals. He said he shared them with his daughter. I then asked him what he'll do when his daughter one day tells him that she agrees with him that the Bible can't be trusted, so she's just going to make up her own morals and reject his.

He looked at me and changed the subject. The bottom line is, if the Bible's not true, there's no basis for right and wrong.

Q. *Since we now have the New Testament, why do we even bother with the Book of Genesis?*

A. I once spoke to a pastor who proudly proclaimed that his was a New Testament church. He said that he didn't have to worry about the Old Testament. So I asked him,

"Pastor, do you believe in marriage?"

"Why yes," he replied.

"Why do you believe in marriage?" I asked.

"Because Paul talks about marriage in the New Testament," he said.

"Well, that's interesting," I said, "because when Paul talks about marriage, such as in Ephesians, he goes back to Genesis to give the foundation for marriage. Do you believe in original sin?"

"Why yes," he said.

"Well that's interesting," I went on. "In 1 Corinthians 15 where Paul's writing about the message of Jesus on the cross and His death and resurrection, he goes back to Genesis to justify why Jesus died on the cross." I continued, "It's all very well to be a New Testament church, but you must realize that all of the New Testament is based in the Old Testament, and ultimately all of this is founded in Genesis 1 through 11."

You see, the first 11 chapters of the Bible are the key to understanding the rest of Scripture. This is how we can fully understand the meaning of New Testament doctrine!

Book of Genesis

Q. *I understand that even secular scientists are now talking about massive catastrophes in regard to the formation of the fossil record. Isn't this what the creationists have been saying all along?*

A. You're right, creationists have always insisted that the fossil record has to be interpreted on the basis of catastrophic events.

When I went to school, my teachers mocked me for believing that the global catastrophe of Noah's flood formed most of the fossil record. They taught that the fossil record formed slowly over millions and millions of years, not quickly.

But now, evolutionary scientists suggest all sorts of global catastrophes to explain, for example, the extinction of dinosaurs. Even in a secular book published recently, leading evolutionists declared that the fossil record now must be understood in terms of catastrophic processes, *not* slow processes as they originally taught.

Why won't they just accept the answer from Genesis that there was a single global catastrophe — the Flood — just thousands of years ago? The real answer's because they don't want to acknowledge that there's a God who judged man's rebellion with a watery catastrophe. It stands as a warning that He will judge again, but next time by fire.

Q. *There are many skeptics who scoff at the account of Noah and the flood. What's their latest argument?*

A. Some evolutionary critics are declaring that you can't build a boat as large as the one Noah constructed from wood. They say that ships have to be made out of steel if they are about 450 feet long.

In a recent issue of our *Creation* magazine, we wrote about some boats that had crews of over 3,000 men built before the time of Christ. And think of all the supplies they would also need to carry. One such ship was probably at least 400 feet long. There's other evidence that huge wooden vessels were built in ancient times that were as large as the biblical ark.

We should remember that the apostle Peter warned us that in the latter days, many will scoff at the Bible (including its account of Noah). Just because we today can't duplicate something that was achieved thousands of years ago, doesn't mean that ancient civilizations didn't have the technology to construct a large ship. I think of the incredible technology behind the Egyptian pyramids that we have difficulty duplicating today.

Remember, these ancient people lived closer to the time of Adam, a man who was created perfect and highly intelligent. Those living closer to Adam would have been more intelligent than people today.

Q. *Don't historians and even many Bible scholars say that writing wasn't invented until about the time of Moses?*

A. Well, you may be surprised when I say this, but I believe Adam could write. And I think the Bible actually states this.

Sadly, we live in a world where we've all been indoctrinated to think in terms of evolutionary ideas. We've been brainwashed to think that people before us weren't as intelligent as we are. As man supposedly developed from a primitive state to a more advanced state, he learned to grunt, then speak, and eventually develop the technology we have today.

But the Bible gives a totally different picture. Man was created intelligent to start with. He had the ability to speak; God had programmed Adam and Eve with a language. Their descendants built musical instruments and cities.

Now listen to the words of Genesis 5:1: "This is the book of the generations of Adam." I believe God's Word here is saying that Adam wrote a book. In fact, I think Adam and his descendants (including Noah and his sons) compiled writings. These were eventually handed down to Moses, who wrote the book of Genesis — all under the inspiration of God's Holy Spirit.

Q. I've heard a number of Christians say that Genesis 1–11 could be symbolic. How would you respond to this?

A. Have you ever read those long lists of "begats" in the Bible? You know, the passages that read this person begat this one, who begat this one, who begat this one and so on. At first they sound rather boring.

But they're the historical records that connect Jesus Christ all the way back in history to the first Adam. They show clearly that all people are descendants of one man — Adam, and that Jesus Christ stepped into history to also be a descendant of Adam, so He could die for us.

Now these genealogies in Genesis are repeated in the books of 1 Chronicles and Luke. As you go back from, say Mary and Joseph, you're able to connect each ancestor with the one before. This goes all the way back through real people until it finally reaches the first person, who is . . . a metaphor? Of course not. The first person was a real human being — Adam.

If Genesis was just metaphor, then how would we know we're all descendants of one man? Why would we be sinners? No, Genesis is not metaphor, but REAL history.

Q. *How could God speak with Adam if he didn't understand the language? Adam must have had a language right from the start. Correct?*

A. Absolutely! We're born with the ability to speak, but our parents teach us a language so we can communicate with each other.

But when Adam and Eve were made, they were mature human beings. Their brain was also mature. God must have programmed them with a language so they could speak to each other and speak to God, understanding everything perfectly.

As you know, the Bible makes it clear there was no death and bloodshed of man or animals before sin. But I've had some Christians claim that there must have been death before Adam — to account for the supposed millions of years of fossils. They then say that Adam would have had to observe death to understand what God meant when he said Adam would die if he ate the fruit he was commanded not to.

But Adam didn't have to observe death to know what the word meant. He was already programmed with a language so that he could speak to God. Adam knew the meaning of every word perfectly from the beginning — including the word "death."

Q. *Surely no Christian would believe the world was full of a horrible disease like cancer before sin, would he?*

A. It's so sad, but, yes, there are many Christians who believe the world was full of cancer before Adam's fall in the Garden. You see, there are many Christians, including many Christian leaders, by the way, who've been brainwashed to believe that most of the fossil record was laid down over millions of years before Adam was created.

Now here's the problem. There are many examples from the fossil record of all sorts of diseases found in the remains of creatures that were fossilized. For example, there are documented examples of tumors in dinosaur bones.

All this means that at the end of the sixth day of creation, when God pronounced everything as very good, for those who believe in millions of years, the fossil record with diseases like cancer, was also pronounced as very good.

This would make God, then, responsible for diseases like cancer. It would also mean that anyone with such diseases should accept them as "very good." This, of course, is terrible. The truth the Bible teaches is that our sin is responsible for the death and disease we see in the world. Disease came after sin, so the fossil record cannot be millions of years old.

Q. *The Bible tells us that Cain went out to the land of Nod. Does that mean there was a land where God had made people other than Adam and Eve?*

A. The land of Nod means "the land of wandering." You see, because of Cain's terrible sin of killing his brother Abel, God told Cain that he would be a "fugitive." Because Adam and Eve had many sons and daughters, no doubt Cain was fearful of what they would do to him for killing their brother.

I've heard many Christians say that God must have created people other than Adam and Eve, because Cain went to the land of Nod and found a wife. Actually, if you read Genesis very carefully, it seems Cain was already married. Cain probably had married one of his sisters, since originally close relatives HAD to marry — which wasn't a genetic or moral problem. After he killed his brother, Cain went away to dwell in this "land of wandering."

It's very important to understand that there was only one man and one woman to start with. You see, all humans are descendants of Adam and Eve, and thus we're all sinners. This is why Jesus could become a man to die for all the descendants of the first couple.

Q. *Because of publications such as the* Scofield Reference Bible, *there are many Christians who believe in the idea of the "gap theory." Does it really matter if Christians accept it?*

A. Well, first let me explain the gap theory.

This idea was developed in the 1800s by church leaders who didn't know what to do with what some scientists were saying about millions of years of history. They popularized the idea that there was a gap of time between the first two verses of Genesis 1. Into this gap, they put a PREVIOUS creation that was destroyed, thus explaining the fossil record of millions of years. According to this view, God then re-created the world in six days.

There are many major problems with this view, including the fact that the gap theory allows death before Adam's sin — and this is contrary to Scripture. Even though the "gap theorists" believe in creation, the danger of their view is that they have based their beliefs from OUTSIDE of Scripture — accepting the evolutionary belief in millions of years, and trying to fit this into the Bible. It's telling people that you can begin outside the Bible and accept man's fallible theories, and use them to interpret the Words of the infallible Creator.

God created everything in six days. There's no room for a gap.

Q. *If mountain climbers need oxygen tanks to climb Mt. Everest, how was Noah able to breathe if his ark floated above the highest mountains?*

A. There are a number of aspects that need to be considered here.

First, mountains like Mt. Everest were not necessarily the height they were during the time of the Flood. In fact, the earth's highest mountains have fossils of sea creatures at their tops, showing they were once under the sea. The sea perhaps rose to cover the mountains, or the mountains were once under the sea and have risen out of the sea, or both things occurred.

Second, measurements indicate that Mt. Everest is currently rising at six inches per year. This movement was probably much greater in the past — particularly at the end of the Flood; so its formation can easily be explained from the time of the Flood.

Thirdly, as the water rose during the Flood, the atmosphere would have risen as well. The difference in pressure for Noah's family would have been equivalent to standing on top of a 100-foot-high building.

Skeptics try to discredit Noah's flood, so it's so important to know how to defend its record in Genesis.

Q. *The Bible tells us that all the land animals that God sent to Noah stayed on the ark for a whole year. How could they have survived cooped up for that long?*

A. This is one of those questions I get asked a lot. If Noah had all of these land animals on board, including dinosaurs, how could he feed and take care of them? In fact, many skeptics challenge Christians with this question to discredit the truth of this account.

Now, the Bible doesn't reveal all the details about what happened on the ark. But we do know that God was in total control of the situation. In fact, I love that verse in Genesis that states, "And God remembered Noah." There's no doubt that God supernaturally looked after the ark and its precious cargo.

Having observed the behavior of animals, we can offer some suggestions. Biologists know that most animals seem to have the ability to hibernate. I suspect that for some animals God supernaturally intensified this ability during the time of the Flood so that the animals' body functions were at a minimum and their food requirements would have been very small. They probably would have slept most of the time. And there may have been other techniques.

Whatever the question, it's vital to believe the Book of Genesis!

Q. *Are there any Bible passages that show us how Jesus Christ viewed the Book of Genesis?*

A. There certainly are. The fact that Jesus quoted directly from Genesis on a number of occasions, treating it as real history, is the reason I take Genesis literally.

The Bible teaches that Jesus is the Truth and the Word. Therefore, He's not going to lead us to believe something is true if it's only a myth or allegory.

For instance, in Matthew 24, Jesus referred to Genesis when reminding people about the story of Noah. He warned them that just as there had been a real judgment by a flood, so there will be coming judgment. Obviously, Jesus treats the event of Noah's flood as a real historical event. He accepted this flood account in Genesis as truth.

Then in Matthew 19, Jesus Christ quoted directly from Genesis about the creation of Adam and Eve. He showed that the meaning of marriage is built on the literal events of Genesis.

And in John 5, Jesus said that if you don't believe the writings of Moses, which included Genesis, then how could you believe His Words? He stated this because all the doctrine He taught was ultimately founded in Genesis. It's absolutely vital that we accept this book.

Q. *I find that many people today scoff at the account of Noah's ark. For example, they say all the land animals couldn't have fit on board. What's the answer?*

A. This is actually a very important question. It can show people that Christians can logically defend their faith and uphold God's Word.

In Genesis 6, we're told that God sent two of every kind of land animal, and seven of some, to Noah. Some skeptics have falsely claimed that Noah would have needed millions of creatures on board.

But Noah only needed representative kinds of animals. For instance, scientists agree that all varieties of dogs that exist today came from the same dog stock — they're all the same kind. In other words, Noah only needed two dogs on the ark. After the ark landed, and as dogs increased in numbers, different groups split off and moved to different places. Eventually, through the process of natural selection, the dog varieties arose.

This is not evolution, but just an example of the inbuilt variability God put in the dog genes in the first place. These principles help us understand that Noah probably needed fewer than 16,000 animals on the ark representing the various kinds. There was plenty of room.

Q: *Why would believing in six literal days of creation be limiting God?*

A. I was on a Christian radio talk show, when a caller accused me of limiting God because I insisted that the days of creation in Genesis 1 were ordinary solar days.

This caller said that she didn't limit God to six days. She allowed Him billions of years to create.

I responded to her by saying that God could do anything He wanted. He could create the universe in six seconds, six minutes, six days, or six billion years. But it's not a matter of what He COULD DO — it's a matter of what He said He DID DO.

I explained to this caller that I didn't limit God in any way, but I did limit myself. I limited myself to letting God tell me what He did from His Word. And if what God tells me in His Word is different to what the world is saying, then the world's theories are wrong!

One of the problems with the Church today, is that instead of limiting ourselves to God's Word for hearing the truth of creation, we limit God to man's fallible theories!

We need to return to getting our answers to the origin of life from the Word of God, instead of from sinful, fallible men.

Q: *Do we really have to believe in the story of the Garden of Eden to be a Christian?*

A. No, but I think it's absolutely vital that Christians accept that there was a real Garden and that all of the Book of Genesis is literally true. Let me explain.

A pastor once approached me at a seminar and said, "You don't have to worry about believing in Genesis! The most important thing is to preach about sin."

I then said to the pastor, "Well, what's sin?"

And he said, "Well you know what sin is!"

"No," I said. "Some pastors are even teaching that it's simply a lack of self-esteem. What is it?"

He told me, "Well, sin is rebellion, rebellion against God."

I then asked him, "Well how do you know it's rebellion? Did you define that yourself, or was it someone else?"

"Well," he said, "if you go back to the Book of Genesis. . . ." and then he realized what he'd said.

You see, if you don't have a literal Garden of Eden with a literal serpent and literal sin, and so on, you don't literally have rebellion. The only way you know what sin is all about is if you accept that the account of the Garden of Eden is literally true.

Q. *How could we ever know whether or not the first woman had red hair?*

A. Well, even though we don't have photos, I'm confident that Eve was not a redhead. How do we know, and why does it matter anyway?

Well, because the Bible teaches us that ALL people are descendants of Adam and Eve, we need to be able to explain why people have different hair color.

Actually, skin and hair color result from the relative levels of two types of melanin pigment: a dark brown pigment, and a reddish version of the pigment. The reason some people have red hair is because they don't have the ability to produce the usual levels of the dark pigment. Because of this, the red pigment of redheads reacts directly with sunlight to produce chemicals that cause damage to their DNA, which can lead to skin cancer.

This inability to produce the dark-brown pigment is probably caused by a mutation, a result of the Curse. Originally, Adam and Eve would have had both types of melanin pigment, so Eve would not have been a redhead!

When we understand about the pigment that gives color to hair and skin, it's easy to defend that ALL people are descendants of Adam and Eve.

Q. *There are still many Christians who believe in some sort of gap between the first two verses of the Book of Genesis. Didn't Jesus Christ himself rule this out?*

A. Absolutely. In fact, if you carefully study the words of Jesus, He made it plain that there can't be a gap of billions of years between Genesis 1:1 and 1:2.

In Mark 10:6, Jesus said, "But from the beginning of the creation God made them male and female." In these words of Jesus, we find that He teaches that Adam and Eve were created in "the beginning of the creation" — NOT after billions of years had passed.

Furthermore, this passage indicates that God had prepared a world for Adam and Eve shortly before — over the five previous days. Also, the expression "beginning of the creation" rules out any second start or "re-creation" as taught by many gap theorists.

The main reason people try to place a gap between the first two verses of Genesis is to accommodate the supposed billions of years for the earth's age.

Jesus made it plain that such a compromise can't be done! And we should follow His understanding and His words because, after all, He is the author of creation and the WORD!

Q. *I know you say that most of the fossil record over the earth is the graveyard of Noah's flood, but is there other evidence consistent with this global catastrophe?*

A. I was sitting recently in a lecture hall listening to meteorologist Mike Oard give an illustrated lecture concerning Noah's flood. It was remarkable.

First of all, he showed massive evidence all over the world for what's called "sheet erosion." You see, if the waters of the global Flood ran off the earth, as the Bible clearly states, we'd expect to see evidence of this.

For instance, when you go to the Grand Canyon, you notice that the area around it is very flat, but every now and then you see sections rising from the flat area consisting of many sedimentary layers. In fact, you find such structures all over the earth.

This is consistent with massive amounts of water causing sheet erosion, taking most of the layers off in sheets but leaving small areas. Because such structures are over massive areas and appear on a global scale, this only makes sense on the basis of Noah's flood.

Second, he showed numerous examples of rivers that run through mountains instead of around them — again, it can only be explained as the Flood waters receded!

Q. *What do you mean when you say that understanding the true meaning of the days of creation is an authority issue? Is it not a language issue?*

A. I certainly agree it's a language issue. After all, the only way words have meaning to us is because we stick to the rules of grammar for a particular language. But I've found that many people, including Christian leaders, want to change the rules when it comes to the meaning of the days of creation.

You see, the word "day" as used in Genesis 1, according to the rules of the Hebrew language, means an ordinary day in that particular context.

Yet I find that even though most theologians agree that the word "day" in Genesis 1 means a 24-hour day, many say it can't mean that because the universe is billions of years old.

By doing this, they're actually saying that the fallible dating methods of fallible man are more important than the actual words of the Bible that God inspired people to write. Thus, they're making man the authority — not God.

This is an authority issue. The Word of God should be read as written and used to judge the fallible words of man — NOT the other way around!

Q. *What's the meaning of the phrase, "after its kind," in Genesis?*

A. This phrase occurs ten times in Genesis 1. I believe God is telling us that He created separate groups of plants and animals, and that one group would not change into another.

If a dog kind could produce a cat kind, or an ape kind could produce a human kind, we'd have evidence for evolution. But we find that dogs produce only dogs, and apes produce only apes. Yes, there can be great variation within each kind, but this has nothing to do with evolution.

In fact, from just one man and woman, there's enough information in their genes that — if it were physically possible — they could have more children than atoms in the entire universe, without having two which looked the same. This same variability exists in all the kinds of creatures God made. To change one kind into a different kind, new information would have to be added into the genes, but this doesn't happen.

Scientists should admit that what we see in the animals fits with what we're told in Genesis: God made each kind to reproduce after its OWN kind.

Q. *Doesn't the Bible tell us that thorns came after the Curse?*

A. You're absolutely right. But for the many Christians who believe the fossil record is millions of years old, they have to accept that the Curse had nothing to do with thorns and thistles.

You see, there are many examples of fossil thorns that are supposed to be millions of years old. Thus, these thorns were allegedly in existence millions of years before the first man existed.

But let's read Genesis 3:17–18, where God said to Adam, "Because thou hast hearkened unto the voice of thy wife, and hast eaten of the tree, of which I commanded thee, saying, Thou shalt not eat of it: cursed is the ground for thy sake; in sorrow shalt thou eat of it all the days of thy life; Thorns also and thistles shall it bring forth to thee; and thou shalt eat the herb of the field."

If God's Word is true, then thorns could not have existed before Adam sinned.

What this means is that Christians who believe God's infallible Word can't believe in man's fallible word of millions of years!

Q. *When I read a book, I always start at the beginning, don't you?*

A. When we buy a book or watch a video, we always start at the beginning. If not, we won't know what the book or movie is all about. If we don't understand the plot, the rest won't make sense.

Well, this is obvious. But, there's one book that most Christians don't start reading at the beginning; they start in the middle or towards the end. It's the Bible!

You see, so many Christians think that the Old Testament is not important today, and that the Book of Genesis could just be myth or allegory. But, it's about time Christians started to wake up and realize that ALL of the New Testament is built on the Old Testament, and ALL of the Old and New Testaments are built on the first 11 chapters of Genesis.

One of the major reasons many Christians don't know how to defend their Christian doctrine is because they don't understand or believe Genesis, the beginning.

Christians need to start being consistent, and read God's Word, beginning with Genesis. If not, they'll never really understand many of the wonderful truths in the rest of God's Word.

Q. *Why would evolutionists be interested in Eve, the first woman?*

A. This is fascinating! In recent years, scientists have conducted a lot of research on DNA that's found in the mitochondria of a cell. Now, this DNA is only inherited through the females. By comparing mutations (or mistakes) in the DNA of people worldwide, scientists came to a startling conclusion. It looks as if all people living today are descended from one woman — and they called her EVE! This has been around in the news for some time, but there's a new startling twist to this research.

Until recently, based upon mutation rates, scientists claimed that this "ancestral Eve" lived hundreds of thousands of years ago. But a recent study claims that the rate of mutations in humans is actually 20 times higher than originally estimated. What does this mean? Using this new figure for mutation rates, the ancestral "mother of all," as they call her, lived a mere 6,000 years ago!

Of course, most scientists don't accept this figure because of their belief in evolution. But isn't it remarkable that this research actually supports Genesis and that the first woman, Eve, was created about 6,000 years ago?

Q. *Six days — why did it take so long?*

A. At many of the meetings I speak at, I often ask people the following questions. "Could the infinite Creator God have created everything in just six minutes?" People of course acknowledge that God could do that. "Well, how about six seconds?" Yes, God could certainly do that. I then ask, "Could He have created in no time at all?" Again, people answer that the infinite Creator could certainly do this.

Then I like to ask this question: "Could God have created everything in six days?" Of course, they have to acknowledge that this could be so.

I then explain to the people that it's not a matter of what God could've done, but what He *said* He did. When you take Genesis 1 as written, the word "day" in context means an ordinary day.

This fits with what God told Moses in Exodus chapter 20 as to why He took six days. This was to be the basis of the seven-day week — six days of work, followed by one day of rest. That's why God took as long as six days to create the universe.

Q. Why did God not create the sun until day 4 of creation?

A. Many people have never thought this through. But you really don't need the sun for day and night. All you need is light from one direction.

The Bible tells us that God made light on day 1. He just doesn't tell us where it came from.

What God HAS told us is that there was light on day 1, which must have come from a temporary source. It was replaced by the sun on day 4. By the way, evolution teaches that the sun existed before the earth, so obviously, one can't accept evolution and add it to the Bible.

I believe that one of the reasons God left the creation of the sun until the fourth day was because He knew that many cultures would want to worship the sun. Remember, God told the Israelites not to worship it as the heathens did. God was showing that HE was the source of all power.

So the answer is so that people would worship the God of the creation, NOT the creation He had made.

Q. *Did Eve really have an extra rib?*

A. Of course, men and women today have the same number of ribs. But this question is about Adam and Eve. If God took a rib out of Adam, did Eve have one more rib than Adam?

Well, at first, she did because Adam had just lost a rib! But ribs have an amazing ability to grow back. The Master Physician has created the human body with a "never-ending supply" of bone — our ribs. Even today, cosmetic surgeons like to use ribs in reconstructive surgery, because they can remove the entire rib from a patient and in the great majority of instances, it will grow back.

There is a membrane covering the outside of all bones. As long as the surgeon leaves this membrane intact, the rib will grow back. If the surgeon needs more bone for later surgery, then he can go back to the same spot and remove the same rib.

It is exciting to realize that Adam did not have to walk around for 930 years with a weakened portion of his rib cage. He had the same number of ribs as his wife. The account of the first couple's "rib surgery" is an amazing testimony about the supernatural origin of the Book of Genesis. Who but God could have known about this special characteristic of ribs?

History of Man

Q. *Are evolutionists saying that preschoolers are no smarter than chimpanzees?*

A. Earlier this year, the Associated Press reported that a chimpanzee performed as well as an average Japanese preschool child on certain "numbers" tests. A chimp can now apparently remember the correct sequence of numbers.

As we've explained in our *Creation* magazine, there's no evolutionary relationship between humans and chimps. Science, for example, shows that the DNA makeup of chimps doesn't offer biological evidence that they're closely related to humans. Even if the DNA showed some similarity, that doesn't mean much at all. Let me give you an example. Is a cloud — made up of almost 100 percent water — somehow related to a watermelon, which is 98 percent water? It's not the similarities that matter, but the significant DIFFER-ENCES between humans and chimps.

Also, you may have seen the story about a parrot that can rival chimpanzees in reasoning ability. But birds aren't supposed to be our close evolutionary cousins, and have much smaller brains than chimps.

Next time you go to a zoo and see a chimpanzee, think about why chimps and apes are somewhat similar to us. We're all the products of the same Designer. But God created people separate from the animals, with incredible mental and communication abilities.

We were created that way so that we could fellowship with our Maker.

Q. *Is it true that our supposed human ancestor, Lucy, may actually be living today?*

A. Yes, and this could be another one of the many embarrassing discoveries for evolutionists!

Villagers on the island of Sumatra have reported seeing an ape-like creature in the jungles. Now, a number of researchers are attempting to find this mysterious creature.

It's described as tailless, shorthaired, and ape-like. It's about 4 feet 6 inches tall, and it walks upright! From casts of its footprints, each foot has four toes in an almost straight row, with a fifth, big toe, jutting to one side.

It just happens that the descriptions and sketches of this creature bear a striking resemblance to those of the australopithecines such as Lucy, the famous supposed ancestor of ours. If this creature in the jungle turns out to be real, it will cause chaos in evolution's ranks. You see, the australopithecines allegedly became extinct millions of years ago.

I'm so glad I have a sure faith in the Word of God that doesn't change. For those who put their trust in man's theories, which change all the time, they must have a very unsettling faith.

Q. *A lot of countries have been developing nuclear weapons lately. People say that if these countries are not careful, they'll blow up the earth and destroy life. Is that possible?*

A. It's certainly true that scientists have developed all sorts of deadly weapons that could wreak havoc on this earth. However, there's something we should ALWAYS keep in mind. No matter what man tries to do, God's in total control.

The Bible tells us that the earth will be blown up one day. Let me explain. In the Book of 2 Peter, we read that there's a fiery judgment to come, when the elements will melt with fervent heat and there'll be a great noise. However, this can't be a description of man destroying himself with nuclear weapons. This is a description of the final judgment by God on this planet.

Just as God judged the wickedness of man in the days of Noah with a global judgment of water, so He'll judge again, but next time by fire!

Because so many people have rejected the truth of God's Word and the fact of creation, they're more fearful of what man can do, instead of fearing the coming judgment of our Creator and Redeemer.

Q. *If scientists ever made life in a test tube, would this be proof of evolution?*

A. First of all, we need to realize that scientists have NEVER made life in a test tube — and I doubt they ever will. But in public school textbooks, students are shown experiments where scientists have been trying to create what they believe were conditions on earth millions of years ago. Then they try to see if they can make life from chemicals.

But what are they really doing? They're using their intelligence to design experiments and complicated pieces of equipment to try and make life to show students that it all happened by CHANCE! Students can see how illogical this is. The scientists aren't using chance — but their intelligence!

Because all of these experiments have failed, some scientists have stated that life didn't evolve on earth after all. They believe that it must have evolved some-where in outer space, and then arrived on earth! They think they have solved the problem about the origin of life, but they have just pushed the problem further out into space!

These scientists could save millions of dollars if only they would read the greatest book of all time, which has the answers we need. That's the Bible, and it starts with Genesis.

Q. *We now know that scientists can clone animals like sheep, but what about dinosaurs? Is this evolution?*

A. First of all, let's understand how scientists clone an animal.

We're all made up of trillions of cells. In nearly all of our cells, we have ALL the information in our genes that made our body. But not all these genes are "switched on" to produce skin cells and so on.

Now take the sheep in Scotland that was cloned. Scientists took the nucleus containing all the genes of a sheep from the cell of a sheep. They placed it in the egg, whose nucleus had been removed, from a female sheep. Now follow this: they then tricked the information from the genes in the nucleus to switch on ALL the genes and develop into a sheep.

Now, you have to have the egg of a female or you can't clone an animal. So the idea of cloning dinosaurs is nonsense unless you also have a LIVING FEMALE DINOSAUR. And cloning is not evolution. No NEW information has been added to the animal — ALL the information came from the genes.

Evolution requires new information to be added. Cloning can only be done because God created the information in the first place.

Q. *Surely you can't be talking about a real ape man being found?*

A. We need to understand that for many people, evolution is more than just a scientific argument about origins. They use it as their philosophy of living, and it impacts every area of their life. Therefore, people who want to reject the Creator are always looking for evidence to support their belief system of evolution.

Christians should be aware that every so-called "missing link" between man and ape has been rejected by scientists. Even many evolutionists throw out Neanderthal man and "Lucy" as our ape-like ancestors. But we shouldn't even have to turn to science to know that these ape-men are false. The Bible clearly tells us that God created everything just as it is, with humans and animals reproducing after their own kind.

What's the REAL missing link? It's people's relationship to the Creator. He made them and He's never been missing. We're made in the image of God and are meant to worship and obey Him. That's the missing link in our society today!

Q. *What would the first man say about our brain power if he were here today?*

A. I don't think we'd like the answer! We tend to think that we're far superior to people who lived before us. We live in an advanced age where we can put men on the moon. But the truth is that man's intelligence has been DECREASING over time. Why? Because sin entered the world. Our brain power is NOT increasing, as evolutionists would expect.

The Bible tells us that the first man and woman had children who went out and built cities and made musical instruments. They were the most intelligent people who ever lived. There's a lot of evidence from archaeology that indicates that even after the Flood, people were able to carry out marvels of technology that we can't duplicate today! I think of the pyramids, for example.

You see, we've been indoctrinated by evolution to think that WE are the most intelligent of all generations. As one man said to me at a seminar, quote, "Genesis was written in simplistic terms so people in the pre-scientific age could understand it." I looked at him and said, "Sir, your brain and mine have suffered from over 6,000 years of the Curse. Actually, Genesis was written in simplistic terms so YOU AND I would understand it!"

Q. *Isn't it amazing that evolutionists recognize that a tremendous amount of intelligence is needed to make a computer, and yet they believe that the incredible complexity of life evolved by chance?*

A. The other day I was looking at some plastic roses, and I thought, *If you gave these to an evolutionary scientist and asked where they came from, he'd probably begin his research by observing the flowers under a microscope. He'd then make these observations: Even though the petals look real, when magnified under the microscope, there are all kinds of imperfections. The edges aren't smooth but jagged, and the color is poorly distributed. No, there are so many imperfections, it's obviously man-made.*

And yet, if the same evolutionist were to put a real rose under the microscope, he'd probably say something like "Yes, the color is perfectly distributed, the edges are beautifully smooth. There are no imperfections. This isn't man-made; this is a product of time and chance. This flower definitely evolved!"

No wonder the Bible states that people are willingly ignorant of the truth! Paul tells us in Romans that the evidence that God created the universe is so great, that if anyone doesn't believe, they are without excuse.

God — not evolution — created life.

Q. *How can we show that human life really does begin at conception? And if we can, would this deeply affect the way people view abortion?*

A. From a biological perspective, human life obviously begins at conception — right when the sperm fertilizes the egg. The fertilized egg has all the information in the genes that make a human being — all the information that makes you. In fact, for the rest of your life, NO new information is ever added. Therefore, it should be obvious that human life begins right at conception.

If everyone knew this, would they stop aborting babies? The answer is no. In fact, I think most evolutionists accept that human life begins at conception, but because they believe in evolution, and thus believe that we're all just animals, to them abortion would be no different than getting rid of rats. The only way for them to change their minds is to accept the first verse of Genesis: "In the beginning God created . . ." and hear the Creator's words in Psalm 51: "In sin did my mother conceive me." Thus, we're sinful humans *right* from conception.

God created us, so abortion is wrong.

Q. *Did ancient man have any advanced technological achievements?*

A. What we find is puzzling to evolutionists who believe that ancient man was primitive. We know that some of these ancients moved huge stones, built monumental structures, and organized complex cultures.

Consider these specific examples: The Gateway to the Sun monument in Mexico was carved out of a single block of volcanic rock that weighed 100 tons, and then it was moved and set in place. No one today knows how they could have accomplished this.

Also consider the Roman temple in Lebanon. It stood on a single foundation stone that had been carefully placed and weighed 2,000 tons! We wouldn't dream of lifting such a weight today!

There are many more such examples that totally defy the evolutionists' picture of primitive man slowly evolving and gaining intelligence!

But none of this would come as a surprise to those who get their answers from Genesis. After all, the first man was highly intelligent. Genesis says that his descendants were building cities and making musical instruments right from the start.

Q. *Was there really an Ice Age?*

A. Yes, there was, although we don't believe in an Ice Age that occurred over millions of years, as the evolutionists teach. We think the Ice Age was a consequence of Noah's flood.

The Bible tells us that fountains of the deep broke open all over the earth at the time of the Flood. This probably means there was also a lot of volcanic action and continental breakup. What would have happened, of course, would be that the Flood waters were warmed by these volcanic explosions. Therefore, you would have warm oceans and a cool land toward the end of the Flood. This would result in a lot of the water being evaporated into the atmosphere.

Well, what's going to happen to it? Because of the tilt of the earth, the wind, and so on, there would have been great storms at the poles; much ice and snow would have been formed. Hundreds of years after the Flood, we believe that this ice accumulated as the Ice Age. Then, as the temperatures of the land and oceans started to stabilize, the ice would have started to melt.

The answer's in Genesis and its account of the Flood!

Q. *Don't most scientists believe that the continents originally consisted of one large landmass?*

A. The interesting thing is that both creationists and evolutionists believe that there was probably only one continent originally. But those who believe in billions of years of earth history think that the continents split up and slowly drifted apart.

From a biblical perspective, when God created the dry land on the third day of creation, it's written that He gathered the waters together into one place. Therefore, the land was probably in one place.

Many creationists believe that this one continent split apart at the time of the Flood just four and a half thousand years ago. We now have some fascinating information coming from a scientist who works at Los Alamos Laboratories in New Mexico. He has the world's most advanced super-computer model for understanding what happens to movements in the earth.

His results show that if a large continent split up, the result would be that the landmasses would be forced apart VERY quickly. All this would also cause the earth to be flooded by water.

This all fits with what the Bible says about Noah's flood. Real science supports the Bible's account of thousands of years of history — not the supposed millions of years.

fossil
facts

Q. *Almost daily we see where scientists have dated something to be millions or billions of years old. Can these dating methods really be trusted?*

A. First of all, most dating methods do NOT show that rocks are millions or billions of years old. You see, there are many ways scientists can try to age-date things. Actually, 90 percent of the dating methods that scientists use give results far younger than evolutionists need.

All dating methods involve something that changes over time. For instance, radioactive uranium, over time, changes into a form of lead. Therefore, if scientists assume they know what was there at the beginning, and that this rate of change has not been disrupted through time, with no contamination, they can calculate how long this has been happening. This is how they get millions of years. But ALL of these assumptions have been shown to be invalid.

Not only this, but other dating methods, such as the amount of salt transported into the oceans, or the amount of helium built up in the atmosphere, indicate that the earth can't be billions or millions of years old.

All dating methods are FALLIBLE, but God's Word, beginning with Genesis, is INFALLIBLE.

Q. *Is there any evidence that fossils can form quickly?*

A. My favorite fossil is a miner's hat. It's rock hard. The hat was found in a mine in Australia where it had been covered with water for more than 50 years. Over that time the minerals in the water turned the soft hat into a hard hat of stone. This is called calcification: solid calcium carbonate replaced the original material in the hat. Today, you can actually see this hat on display in a mining museum in Tasmania.

I jokingly tell children at our seminars that this fossil is "frightening." Well, the children let me know that it isn't frightening at all. I then tell them that it might not scare them, but I believe it's frightening to an evolutionist. You see, it shows that creation scientists are correct when they say that fossils and rocks don't take thousands or millions of years to form!

There are many other examples like this that show us that most of the fossil record was formed 4,500 years ago by the event of Noah's flood — NOT by slow process over millions of years as evolutionists insist!

Q. How can extinct fossils still be living?

A. It all started in my homeland of Australia, at the Riversleigh fossil deposits in North West Queensland.

Scientists found some fossils of turtles that they thought had become extinct during the so-called Pleistocene period. This was about 50,000 years ago, according to the evolutionary time scale. Then, about 90 kilometers (56 miles) away, they found a new species of a living turtle. It turns out that this turtle appears to be the same as the fossils they found!

The remarkable thing was that the living turtles showed absolutely no signs of any evolutionary changes over the supposed 50,000 years since the fossils were formed.

This turtle is just another example of a living specimen that appears to be identical to the fossils that supposedly formed many thousands, or sometimes millions, of years ago according to evolution. We call these "living fossils."

If most of the fossils we find today are the result of a worldwide flood that occurred in the days of Noah, then you would expect to find many of the same animals alive today. And this is what we do see. It fits with Genesis.

Q. *How can scientists investigate life's origins, when they can't go back in time?*

A. It's a big problem. Now think about this. In 1995 we saw a murder trial involving a famous athlete that went on for many, many months. Now if lawyers and the forensic scientists had such a hard time trying to reconstruct an event that occurred just months earlier, how can scientists ever reconstruct what happened supposedly millions or billions of years ago?

Imagine that I have an evolutionary scientist with me right now and we are talking about science. Would we argue about photosynthesis, how a computer works, or how to put up a space shuttle? We wouldn't disagree about these things. But would we argue about our origins? Most definitely!

So what's the difference? Well, current technology deals with what we can observe IN THE PRESENT; these are the things we agree about. But, when it comes to origins and the past, this is OUTSIDE real science because we don't have the past with us!

In Genesis, though, we have a record of a witness who has been there in the past. This is the basis for TRUE science.

Q. *How can dinosaur bones have blood cells? Aren't they all fossilized?*

A. Now this is a fascinating story. A team of scientists from Montana State University examined the bones of a nearly complete *T. rex*. They were surprised to find that some parts deep inside the huge leg bone weren't completely fossilized. Here's the question: "How could unfossilized dinosaur bones remain for millions of years?"

Not only this, but even more startling, when the scientists examined thin sections of the bone under a microscope, they found what appeared to be red blood cells. This really surprised them, since these cells are made mostly of water. They usually break apart shortly after the death of an animal anyway. At first they couldn't believe they'd found red blood cells, because there's no way they could survive for millions of years.

They did a lot more testing, but all their tests indicated that they really had found *T. rex* blood cells.

So now we have fresh *T. rex* bone with red blood cells still intact. How could this be?

Genesis tells us the solution. This world is NOT millions of years old. Also, dinosaurs like *T. rex* didn't die out millions of years ago but lived in the world after the Flood, possibly until very recent times.

It's great to know that God's Word explains the evidence!

Q. *Evolutionary scientists say that the fossils in the rock layers are millions of years old. How do they date these fossils to get such OLD dates?*

A. Well, you may find this hard to believe, but the fossils date the rocks that they're in, and the rocks date the fossils they're in! Let me explain.

The main evidence for evolution is the fossil record. Supposedly, this is a record of the evolution of life, with the oldest and simplest creatures at the bottom and the younger and more complex forms at the top.

These fossil sequences are actually based on a belief that the earth is millions of years old. And the geologic ages of millions of years have been built upon the basis that the idea of evolution occurring over millions of years is true. Now you might say, BUT this is circular reasoning! Well it sure is. In fact, evolutionary thinking is full of that kind of circular reasoning.

When I went to college, my biology professors told me the geologists had the evidence for evolution. But my geology professors told me the biologists had the evidence for evolution. In reality, the evidence doesn't fit with evolution, but it DOES fit with what the Bible records in Genesis.

Q. *Has anyone conducted any experiments to try to test whether fossils could really last millions of years?*

A. That's a good question. Of course, no one can observe what could have happened over millions of years. But there are some observations in the present that do call into question the belief that fossils can be preserved that long.

Many people may have heard of the famous Laetoli footprints that evolutionist Mary Leaky found in Tanzania. These are supposed to be 3.5 million years old — and they look very human by the way! The trail of prints was preserved in volcanic ash.

Two years after the trail was discovered, concerns about the erosion of the prints caused scientists to cover them to protect the prints from the elements. Since then, it's still eroded further, and has been damaged by tree roots. The government is attempting to preserve the tracks again by removing these roots and reburying the trail.

When you think about it, if so much natural damage can be done to the tracks in only 20 years, it really calls into question the claim that they survived undamaged for almost 200,000 TIMES that length of time! But Genesis makes it clear — the world is not that old.

Q. *Excuse the pun, but a fossil clock sounds like something "trapped in time!" Tell us about this fascinating artifact!*

A. Because of the intense evolutionary indoctrination we've received, most people assume that it takes millions of years for sediment, like sand or mud, to harden into rock. But given the right ingredients, this can happen quickly. Mixing cement is an obvious example.

In our *Creation* magazine, we showed a picture of the mechanism of a clock encased in solid rock, along with seashells. Now, no one believes this clock was made millions of years ago. The clock was found in 1975 near a jetty at Westport, Washington. We know there have been many shipwrecks in this area.

Obviously, the right mix of sand and other substances hardened around this clock, making it look like a clock in hard rock!

There really is nothing spectacular about this at all — this sort of thing happens all the time in different parts of the world. But the average person doesn't usually hear about such things, and thus goes on thinking that rocks and fossils must take millions of years to form.

This "clock in the rock" will eventually be displayed in our creation museum near Cincinnati, Ohio, where we'll be teaching people the truth about the history of the world from the Bible.

Q. *What fossil was found in the wrong place at the wrong time?*

A. You know, you quickly realize how fragile the idea of evolution is when just one tiny jawbone can send shock waves through evolutionist circles.

Scientists found a tiny jawbone in Australia that was supposedly 115 million years old. This bone belonged to a placental mammal. But according to evolutionists, such mammals weren't supposed to be in Australia until a mere five million years ago. Thus, according to the evolutionists' own theory, this jawbone is 105 million years TOO EARLY! It's in the wrong place at the wrong evolutionary time!

This is just one more clue that should make it obvious to everyone that there's something dreadfully wrong with evolutionary theory. In fact, the ONE unchanging truth about evolutionary theory is that IT'S ALWAYS CHANGING. This is because evolution is NOT science — it's a belief.

There is good news, though. The account of creation in the Book of Genesis never needs changing to explain the real facts of science. People need to get their answers from Genesis instead of from the ever-changing theories of fallible humans!

Q. *The evolutionists tell us that the fossil record is one of their best evidences for evolution. How do creationists explain these layers of fossils?*

A. I'm always amazed that people don't think logically when they hear evolutionists explain how they think the fossil record formed.

I'll never forget the illustration found in my old biology textbook about fossilized fish. The evolutionist authors had drawn pictures to explain to the students that when fish died, they sank to the bottom, and then were slowly covered by mud. Then over millions of years, layers of fish fossils formed.

But most fish float when they die. And by the time they get to the bottom, they're already falling apart — or have been eaten by scavengers. Every time I've gone diving on the Great Barrier Reef in Australia, I haven't seen dead fish on the ocean floor waiting to be fossilized! It takes special circumstances to quickly cover and preserve these creatures' remains if they're to turn into fossils.

How do you explain billions of fossils in layers, sometimes miles thick over much of the earth? The catastrophic global flood of Noah's day, just thousands of years ago, would have buried billions of creatures, and preserved them as fossils.

Evolution and the Dinosaurs

Q. *I've never seen the word "dinosaur" in the Bible, yet you say that they're mentioned in the Scriptures?*

A. Well, the term "dinosaur" was only invented in 1841 by an Englishman named Sir Richard Owen. The Bible I use was translated into English in 1611, so you wouldn't expect to find the word "dinosaur" in my Bible.

But in the Book of Job, there is a description of a great beast called behemoth, which I believe was a dinosaur.

It had a tail like a cedar tree and bones as strong as pieces of brass. His strength was in his loins. The great creature lay in the reeds and drank up the river. He was the "chief of the ways of God," which means he was the largest animal God made. This animal couldn't have been an elephant or hippo, which have small tails. In fact, the only animal that fits this description is a dinosaur.

Now this behemoth, or dinosaur, was also living at the same time as Job, because God said to Job, "BEHOLD the behemoth." According to evolutionists, though, dinosaurs died out millions of years before man.

But God made the first behemoth on the sixth day of creation, just a few thousand years ago.

Q. *Could there really be dinosaurs (such as those in the Jurassic Park movies) alive somewhere in the world today?*

A. I believe it's possible. In fact, there have been reports over the years that creatures whose descriptions fit that of some dinosaurs have been seen.

In 1919, there were rumors of a huge animal seen in the African Congo. The description of this creature fits with a sauropod dinosaur. Reports even continued into the 1980s. In fact, a team led by an evolutionary scientist traveled to the area to see if they could photograph this creature. The members of the expedition claimed to have seen the animal and recorded its roar, but they weren't able to get a picture.

Of course, most evolutionary scientists are very skeptical about such reports anyway. They don't, of course, believe dinosaurs ever lived at the same time as people.

There are also reports from around the world of dinosaur-like creatures such as the Loch Ness Monster in Scotland and Ogo Pogo in Canada.

Now, would creationists be surprised if scientists discovered a living dinosaur? No. God created all the land animals alongside Adam and Eve.

Q. *Did Alexander the Great see a dinosaur?*

A. In one of my favorite 19th century commentaries I use for Bible study, I came across an interesting reference from an old history book. Let me read the quote to you:

"Aelianus speaks of a dragon in India, which, when it perceived Alexander's army near at hand, gave such a prodigious hiss and blast, that it greatly frightened and disturbed the whole army."[1]

As I often state in my lectures on dinosaurs, I believe that many of the dragon legends of old could be accounts of encounters with large animals that today we call dinosaurs. Many of the descriptions of the dragons in the old history books fit with the descriptions of some of the dinosaurs like *T. rex*, *Stegosaurus*, and so on.

It wouldn't surprise me at all if Alexander came across a live dinosaur, referred to in his day as a dragon. From a biblical perspective, dinosaurs and people lived at the same time as land animals. Also, they were made on the same day as Adam and Eve. So it wouldn't surprise those who believe the Bible that Alexander possibly met a real dinosaur.

---

1. John Gill, *An Exposition of the Old and New Testament* (London, 1809), Vol. 9; revised and updated by Larry Pierce, 1994–1995.

Q. Did dinosaurs really exist?

A. Dinosaurs are real. I remember after I'd preached in a church in Australia and was in the pastor's car. The pastor's son piped up and said, "Hey, dad, how come you told us dinosaurs never existed?"

"Quiet, son," said the pastor.

You see, because he thought that dinosaurs and evolution went hand-in-hand, and that Christians didn't have answers to explain dinosaurs, he just told his son they didn't exist. But what happens when you take your son to a large museum and you see the bones of these creatures? Obviously, they DID exist.

They AREN'T a mystery, and they can easily be explained on the basis of the Bible. Did you know that the Bible talks more about dinosaurs than just about any other animal? You see, the word "dinosaur" was first used in 1841. The King James Version was first translated in 1611. That's why you don't find the word "dinosaur" in the Bible. Before these creatures were named dinosaurs, they were called "dragons." That word occurs a number of times in the Old Testament.

Yes, dinosaurs did exist . . . and not so long ago.

Q. *Did dinosaurs really eat rocks?*

A. Let me explain. Many of the huge dinosaurs, like *Apatosaurus* and *Ultrasaurus,* had very few teeth to chew plants. Now being as large as they were, they would have starved to death by the time they tried to chew enough food to digest.

But scientists have found numbers of smooth, polished stones within the rib cages of many large vegetarian dinosaurs. They believe that the dinosaurs swallowed the stones to help them grind the food that they must have swallowed whole. You know, alligators and many birds today use stones in the digestive tract to grind up food that's swallowed whole.

As with birds and alligators, the large dinosaurs would surely have starved to death without the stones. I often wonder that if evolution is true, how many dinosaurs, alligators, and birds starved to death until they some-how "learned" that they needed to swallow rocks in order to digest their food?

When you start with Genesis, you quickly realize how foolish it is to believe in evolution. All the many com-plexities of life should make us truly marvel at the God of creation and His infinite wisdom.

Q: *You've refuted evidence that dinosaurs evolved into birds before, but what more can you add?*

A. At a gathering of dinosaur experts in Philadelphia, a number of papers were presented about this famous fossil called *Sinosauropteryx.* One of the papers declared that the so-called feathers were probably just collagen fibers beneath the skin of a reptile. It was even shown that this same type of fibering appears in lizards.

Now, the fascinating thing about all this was to observe the reactions to this research by some of the evolutionists in the audience. Many of them became angry. You'd think they'd been personally attacked! Actually, what really happened was that their religion of evolution had been shaken.

You see, evolutionists SO want evolution to be true, they're desperate for anything — even "feathered" dinosaurs, something they can cling to in their efforts to reject God's Word.

You know what's thrilling to me? God's Word has never changed! Genesis states that God made the birds BEFORE the reptiles. So don't put your trust in man's theories!

Q. *Haven't most evolutionists accepted the theory that dinosaurs became extinct because of an "asteroid impact" that supposedly occurred 65 million years ago?*

A. The idea of an asteroid to explain dinosaur extinction is certainly the most popular view among evolutionists. But this has come under criticism from the collections manager of the Ohio University's Orton Geological Society. This scientist insists that the evidence just doesn't add up.

He points out that of the 285 species of dinosaurs, only about 16 to 18 are found at the supposed time of the extinction. This means that most dinosaurs died out well before this alleged event! He also makes the point that in the evolutionary time scale of things, other animals lived through this time in geologic history. They weren't affected at all by the impact. And another thing: he argues that the evidence indicates there have been many other large meteorite or asteroid impacts in history that DIDN'T cause extinctions.

Actually, all he's doing is making public the kind of things creationists have been saying all along.

The evolutionist answer to dinosaur extinction doesn't make sense, but Genesis does make sense of dinosaur history.

Q. *Do some Christians believe that dinosaurs never existed?*

A. Because some Christians don't know how to explain things like dinosaur bones, they have actually said to me that maybe God made these fossils to test our faith. Well, the Bible states that God is "not a man that He should lie." God is truth. God wouldn't deceive us in any way. Unfortunately, some people, because they've not understood dinosaur bones, have tried to explain them by saying that God put them in the ground.

If Christians would only read their Bible, starting with Genesis, they can understand dinosaurs. First of all, their bones speak of death. The Bible teaches that there was NO death of animals before man. God described His creation as "very good." If there were billions of dead bones under the Garden of Eden, this would totally contradict Genesis. Genesis 3 declares that death, bloodshed, disease, and suffering came into the world only AFTER Adam sinned. Thus, dinosaur bones have to fit in the Bible after sin.

Genesis also tells us that the world was destroyed by a flood in Noah's day, which would have buried lots of animals. You see, starting with Genesis we can account for dinosaur bones!

Q. *Were dragons real creatures?*

A. There are flood legends that have come down from many different people groups around the world, and many of these legends are very similar to the Bible's account of creation and the Flood.

For instance, the Australian Aborigines, before they even met missionaries, had stories about a global Flood, three sons in a boat and many other similarities to the Bible's account. The same can be said of the American Indians, Fijians, Eskimos — in fact cultures all around the world.

The reason for this is that these people are all descendants of Noah. They handed down the story of the Flood to succeeding generations. The stories changed over the years, but the similarities to the Bible are still there.

I believe the same sort of thing happened with dragon legends. These stories are based on real encounters with real beasts. The stories exist all over the world, handed down from their forefathers.

What were the dragons? When you read about the descriptions of many of these dragons in the old history books — you suddenly realize they fit many of the descriptions we have today for DINOSAURS. Yes, dragons were probably dinosaurs!

Q. *What about flying dragons? Aren't they just mythical?*

A. Well, the pictures of flying dragons we see in movies and books may be a bit fanciful. But I believe they are based on memories from people who DID see such flying creatures, probably flying reptiles like the pterodactyls.

In the fifth century before Christ, Herodotus, the famous Greek historian, wrote about the "winged serpents" of Arabia. Their descriptions fit what we know about pterodactyls. Similar reports of such creatures come from Ethiopia and India. And there are people living today in the jungles of Southern Africa who say they've seen flying reptiles. They call them "kongamato."

Even the Bible talks about flying serpents that lived beside people. They're found in the Book of Isaiah.

Now evolutionists insist that the flying reptiles became extinct with the dinosaurs millions of years ago. But the Bible and old history books give evidence that such creatures lived with people, and not so long ago.

And it certainly wouldn't surprise those who believe in the Book of Genesis if such a flying reptile was still alive somewhere on the earth today. After all, the Bible says that God created all the land animals on the sixth day of creation.

Q. *How should Christians respond to movies that have a lot of evolutionary content to them?*

A. Let's look at Disney's film *Dinosaur*. Although the movie doesn't have as much evolution on the surface as the *Jurassic Park* films did, it's there nonetheless.

In fact, the main theme of *Dinosaur* is that the key to "survival of the fittest" is to be compassionate and cooperative. So rather than portraying the violent Darwinian "struggle for survival," the movie's theme is that cooperation is essential to stay alive. The movie really presents a sanitized version of evolutionary thinking. But Darwinian evolution is really a violent view of nature. It was once described by Tennyson as "nature, red [with blood] in tooth and claw."

If you understand the Bible's timeline of history, it's quite easy to explain dinosaurs. The Bible says that all land animals, including dinosaurs, were made on day 6 of creation, along with man. Dinosaurs did not die out millions of years before man, which is the story of evolution. There is much evidence that dinosaurs were living in the past few thousand years.

Christians need to present this Bible-defending information to their family and friends. When they do, they'll be surprised to learn that dinosaurs can be a wonderful tool with which to share the gospel.

Q. *Is the disappearance of the dinosaurs really that puzzling of a mystery?*

A. Well, I frankly get tired, at times, telling people there's really no mystery about what happened to the dinosaurs. You see, most people think that what happened to the dinosaurs must be different to anything that's occurred to other animals. But it's not!

I live near the Cincinnati Zoo. It has one of the world's leading endangered species programs. If I asked the scientists there questions like, "Why do you have an endangered species program?" they would answer something like this: "Because of man's clearing the land, pollution, lack of food, and so on, lots of species have become extinct and are therefore lost forever. We need the endangered species program to stop this from happening."

If you then ask the question "What happened to the dinosaurs?" the answer would be something like, "We don't know. It's a big mystery." Actually, what happened to the dinosaurs is that we didn't start our endangered species programs early enough!

The answer's simple and comes from Genesis — because of sin and the Curse and the event of the Flood — lots of changes have occurred on this earth. They've caused many animals, including the dinosaurs, to die out!

Q. *Weren't most of the mammoths killed in some sort of catastrophe that froze many of them with the grass still in their mouths?*

A. Actually, this is the prevalent belief I find among many Christians today. But this idea is very wrong.

Michael Oard is a meteorologist; he studies weather, past and present. He's been working on the problem of how to explain the extinction of the wooly mammoths in Siberia for many years. He's found some startling things that have caused creation scientists to rethink their theories concerning these large, elephant-like animals.

Mike found that only a handful of carcasses were actually frozen. But there are millions of bones of mammoths. He also found that, for the most part, they're buried in wind-laid sediments.

He believes that as the Ice Age (which was caused by Noah's flood, by the way) began to recede, dramatic climate changes occurred. During the Ice Age, grasses that would have been food for mammoths were growing in Siberia. As the climate changed, great dust storms occurred, burying many of them, which is why we find their bones today.

Secular scientists are perplexed by the mammoths. But a model based on the Bible's account of the Flood explains exactly what we observe today!

Q. *In Job 40 we read about a huge creature called behemoth. What animal do you think this was?*

A. Well, some Bible commentaries and Bible study notes say that behemoth was perhaps an elephant or rhinoceros. I have to shake my head when I read these notes. The text of the Bible makes it clear it could NOT have been any of these animals.

If you read the description of behemoth, you'll realize quickly that it was a very large animal — in fact the largest God made. Also, it had a big tail that is described as moving like a cedar tree. So it's not an elephant or rhino. Their tails look like pieces of rope just dangling in the wind! Also, they're NOT the largest land animals.

We know that the largest land animal that ever existed was a dinosaur. This fact, together with the description that behemoth moved its tail like a cedar tree, makes me think of the great dinosaur called *Brachiosaurus*.

Sadly, because many Christians have been taught evolution, they think dinosaurs lived millions of years BEFORE man. If we get rid of our false evolutionary ideas, it makes so much sense to say that behemoth was a dinosaur!

Creation
Evidence
in Nature

Q. *If the earth is only thousands of years old, as creationists believe, why do the guides at Carlsbad Caverns talk about stalactites and stalagmites forming over millions of years?*

A. Actually, there's a lot of evidence indicating that they could have formed very quickly.

I recently went to the Katherine Caves in the northern part of Australia. On a tour, I was told by the guide that it took millions of years to grow stalactites, hanging from the roof of the cave, because this cave hardly had any water in it at all. Then he showed us an area where vandals in the 1900s had destroyed a number of the stalactites. As we were about to move on to the next cave, I asked whether or not the stalactites we were looking at were the ones that had been damaged by the vandals. He said yes.

I then asked him whether what I was looking at were "re-growths." Yes, he said. I then said, "But this re-growth is up to six inches long. That certainly didn't take millions of years." He glanced at the stalactites, then stared at me, and didn't know what to say. We just moved on!

How do creationists explain limestone caves? It's all to do with Noah's flood and lots of water!

Q. *I've seen pictures of elephants swimming, but are they really "super swimmers?"*

A. Well, according to evolutionists, they must have been INCREDIBLE swimmers.

We've certainly seen elephants swim across rivers and lakes, but not hundreds of miles across the open ocean. But this is what believing in evolution requires.

You see, according to the evolutionary time scale of events, the land bridge that joins North and South America supposedly formed about 2-1/2 to 3-1/2 million years ago. But follow this: evolutionists say the fossil record gives evidence that elephants crossed from North America to South America more than 6 million years ago. According to their own dates, there wasn't any land bridge at this time!

When evolutionists are asked how the elephants made the journey of hundreds of miles without a land bridge, they say they must have swam across!

I'm so glad I get my answers from the Bible and don't have to resort to such ridiculous ideas. The Ice Age as a result of the Flood would have caused land bridges all around the earth because water was turned into ice. This would have made it easy for animals to move around the earth.

Biblical creationists have logical answers to what often seem hard questions!

Q. *Is someone saying our purpose in life is to serve bacteria?*

A. Well, according to some evolutionists, humans are here to provide a good place for bacteria to live and feed upon.

In an issue of *Veggie Life*, we read the following: ". . . humans evolved merely to provide food and shelter for bacteria. After all, bacteria are the original life form. They existed long before there were plants and animals and they've changed little in billions of years."

So, according to at least one evolutionist, we're really nothing but a food bag for bacteria. Now THAT must make people think they've got REAL purpose and meaning in life! No wonder evolutionary ideas make young people wonder if their lives have any meaning.

You wonder how people can be so blind. Humans can think, write music, engineer great buildings — and yet they're not considered as great as bacteria!

We're NOT inferior to bacteria. Genesis tells us that we're very special — we're made in the image of God. And even though sin has marred everything, because of what Jesus Christ did on the cross of Calvary, we can have fellowship with our Creator.

Q. *Why are kangaroos found only in Australia?*

A. Now, this may surprise lots of people, but kangaroos have lived in many other parts of the world!

At our Answers in Genesis seminars, I like to ask our audience, "How many of you believe kangaroos once lived in the Middle East? NO ONE puts up his hand. Then I ask, "How many believe that Noah's flood was a real event?" The hands go up.

"How many believe that Noah's ark was a real boat?" Yes, they agree on that, too. "How many believe that two of every kind of land animal, including the kangaroos, went on the ark?" Yes, they accept that.

Then I ask, "How many people believe the ark landed in the Middle East?" Up go the hands. "How many now believe that kangaroos came off the ark after the Flood?" They start to laugh and put up their hands.

Then I ask, "Did kangaroos once live in the Middle East?" *All* the hands now go up.

You see, when we think with a biblical perspective, we realize that ALL the kinds of land animals must have once lived in the Middle East because they came off Noah's ark.

Q. *Isn't "two heads are better than one" a true cliché?*

A. Well actually, I'm not talking about two people using their minds to solve a problem. In this instance I'm referring to a two-headed calf!

Our local newspaper had a report and photograph of a calf that looked normal from the neck down. However, it had two heads, two mouths, four eyes and three ears. Anyone looking at this would recognize it as a mutation. Something obviously went wrong with the genetic information as the calf was developing. This is NOT an improvement!

Now what's the point of all of this? Well, mutations are nothing more than mistakes. Although not all mutations are as bad as this, nonetheless mutations ARE downhill changes. And the fact is that one of the basic mechanisms for evolution is that some mutations are supposed to enable an organism to evolve onwards and upwards.

The next time you hear someone defend evolution, remember the two-headed calf and ask yourself this question, "Could a series of mistakes really help organisms to evolve?" Then think of the answer in Genesis: the infinite Creator created the information for life. Man's sin brought judgment and the Curse, which has resulted in mutations!

Q. *Can chimps really be taught to communicate as we do?*

A. After years of experiments in training chimps, I believe we can honestly say that no one has ever demonstrated that chimps have true grammatical ability — much to the frustration of evolutionists.

On the other hand, it's been shown that human babies instinctively grasp the structure of any language. This confirms that humans, but not animals, were created to speak. A fascinating example of this "inborn" language ability comes from Nicaragua, in Central America.

About 500 deaf children were placed in communities. According to *Discover* magazine, these deaf children began to "talk" to each other with a full sign language that emerged from nowhere! This language had the elements of grammar, a full vocabulary, and everything you'd expect in a language!

This is exactly what creationists would expect. God created the first man, Adam, already programmed with a complex language, the ability to communicate with God and man. All humans have inherited this ability from Adam. We're all "wired up" for it! Evolutionists can't explain this.

Chimps will never be able to learn a language as human beings can. They weren't created for it!

Q. *Is it true that man is basically a religious creature and has a knowledge of God, even if he is not taught about God?*

A. In Genesis 1:26 we read, "And God said, Let us make man in our image, after our likeness." And again in Genesis 1:27 we read, "So God made man in his own image, in the image of God created he him: male and female created he them."

Being created in God's image makes us "God-oriented" beings with a built-in knowledge of Him. Also, Paul teaches us in Romans that God has written on our hearts the fact that He exists.

Let me give you a marvelous example.

Helen Keller was born blind and deaf, and for years had no way to communicate with anyone. Finally, people found a way. One day, a pastor was brought in to teach her about Christianity. When he started telling her about God, she responded with excitement. Although I'm not sure she received the Lord as her Savior, she had always known that God existed. She just didn't know what to call Him.

Regardless of whether Helen Keller actually trusted Christ as Savior, it's obvious that even someone born blind and deaf can know that God exists. We're made in His image and therefore bear knowledge of Him.

Q. *Are there really some fish that can actually change their sex?*

A. It's remarkable, but true!

One example is the giant sea bass found in the oceans. From the time it hatches until it reaches about 300 pounds, it is a male. Then it starts to undergo a transformation. By the time it reaches about 400 pounds, it is a female and remains that way until it dies. There are other fish that do this as well.

This presents an impossible challenge for the evolutionists to explain. Were all of the first ones that evolved males? What made them change sex? If there were no females at first until they all reached a certain size, then how did they reproduce? These are just some of the questions about the giant sea bass that the evolutionists can't answer.

When we turn to the Bible, we read that God created all of the fish and the other things that swim in the seas on day 5 of creation. Therefore, we'd say that they were wonderfully designed to undergo this unusual change right from their first appearance on the earth.

Q. How can you have a good mutation if it's going in the wrong direction?

A. First of all, let me explain the word "mutation." In the cells of animals, plants, and humans are genes. These contain the information, or blueprints if you like, that build each organism. Now a mutation occurs when there's a copying mistake; for example, something like ultraviolet light causes a change in one or more of these genes.

Evolutionists claim that these changes over millions of years help to cause organisms to evolve. But the changes that occur are actually the OPPOSITE of what's required of evolution.

For example, there is a winged beetle that lives on large continental areas. But on one particular windy island, the same beetle has NO wings. A mutation occurred in the genes of the beetle that caused it to lose the information for wings. Evolutionists say that this mutation was beneficial. They contend that the beetle would be blown into the sea and drowned if it had wings.

Now while this may be true for the beetles living on the island, the point is, the beetle has LOST information. For evolution to occur, organisms would need to obtain NEW information for their genes.

The reason for mutations is found in Genesis. Because of the Curse, things tend to degenerate — not improve, as evolutionists would tell us.

Q. *I recently read an article declaring that flowers developed color because of the vision of bees. What's wrong with that wild idea?*

A. In the article to which you refer, it was stated that bees existed millions of years before the flowering plants. The article says that bees had to have the same color vision millions of years ago, as they do now. Therefore, as the flowering plants began to evolve, the flowers "chose" their colors in accordance with the colors that the bees could see. This made the flowers better adapted to being pollinated by the bees.

This is clearly a ridiculous idea. How can a flower choose its own color? The same people who say that the universe can't have an intelligent Designer, are now trying to say that plants have some sort of intelligence that allows them to choose their color!

Plants are NOT intelligent! Furthermore, the first chapter of Genesis declares that flowers were created on day 3 and the bees on day 6. Flowers came BEFORE the bees. This is OPPOSITE to what evolutionists teach.

Whenever it comes to finding the truth about nature, we need to remember to always to turn to God's Word, beginning with Genesis.

Q. *Does it take millions of years for coral reefs to form?*

A. Well, if Noah's flood occurred only about 4,500 years ago, as the Bible indicates, then the coral reefs, such as the famous Great Barrier Reef in Australia, *must* be less than 4,500 years old.

When I went to school, though, my teachers were adamant that because coral grew so slowly, it would take millions of years for a reef structure to form. But I remember the first time I took a trip out to the Barrier Reef and went into one of the underwater observatories. I was amazed to see great clumps of coral already growing on the large anchor chains! This had certainly not taken millions of years.

Then, I'd heard about some fascinating research on coral growth conducted by Australian scientists. They found that the average growth of certain corals was over a half an inch per year. Now, the deepest part of the Great Barrier Reef is around 180 feet. At this growth rate, the entire reef could be explained in less than four thousand years, which fits the biblical date of the Flood!

Yes, the Bible can be trusted from its very first verse!

Q. Aren't the differences in breeds of dogs really evolutionary changes?

A. No, they aren't! Sadly, too many students in our schools have been taught that the different types of dogs are proof of evolution.

Many years ago I was a science teacher in Australia's public schools. This is how I explained these changes to my students: "See these animals here? What are they? Well, they're dingoes, coyotes, fox, collies, great Danes, little Chihuahuas, St. Bernards, and poodles. Okay, students, what do we call those animals?"

"Well, they're called dogs, sir."

"All right, so what were they?"

"Dogs."

"Well, what are they today?"

"Dogs."

"What will they be tomorrow?"

"Dogs."

"Well, students, do you think that's evolution?"

"Well, no sir. They're just dogs."

The students were right. You start with dogs, and you finish with dogs.

You see, if evolution were true, you should have dogs changing into something totally different. And that's exactly what you don't see. God created distinct kinds of animals, but with great variation within each.

Q. *Are evolutionists now saying that the human brain has evolved as far as it can?*

A. Scientists in England have discovered something, and what they say is remarkable. By looking at the balance between the nerve cells and the nourishing blood vessels in our brain, they came to a startling conclusion: It seems that our brains are at the maximum information-processing capability possible.

One scientist even stated that it would be "hard to improve" on what evolution had already achieved.

Well, since the Bible tells us that the brain did not evolve, but was made by the living God in whose image we're made, then we shouldn't be surprised at all when we find that the brain looks like it was designed in the best way possible!

I have students often ask me, "Sir, if it's so obvious that God created the world and all its creatures, why don't all the scientists believe it?"

Of course the answer is that it really is a spiritual question. Man is in rebellion against his Creator, and, even though the evidence is obvious, he doesn't want to believe and thus acknowledge that God owns us and therefore He sets the rules.

Q. *How in the world does a butterfly use the sun for navigation?*

A. Scientists from the University of Arizona have demonstrated that monarch butterflies align themselves with the sun in making their incredible 2,400-mile migration across North America. Now THIS is a skill that many pilots wish they had!

The amazing thing is that the ability to use the sun as their compass is based upon some type of internal clock. For example, when the butterflies were kept in darkness for six hours and then released, they flew west-northwest instead of the normal south-southwest direction. That's because their internal clocks had been "reset."

The scientists were also impressed by the monarch's ability to stay on course on overcast days, indicating they may even have a type of "magnetic compass" that they rely on.

In Genesis we read that the sun was to be used for signs and seasons. Maybe these signs and seasons weren't just for humans, but also for animals like the butterflies.

Evolutionists have no explanation for the monarch's abilities, but when we get our answers from the Bible, it's just another wonder of our great Creator!

Q: *How can chickadees withstand cold temperatures without extra body fat?*

A. Because chickadees are fairly small birds, they have a high rate of body activity. This requires them to eat a large amount of food. But unlike similar-size birds such as finches that build up fat reserves for the winter, chickadees don't build up any such reserves at all. This means they must have a constant supply of food.

Now in the northern parts of the world, the winter nights can be quite long and cold, making it tougher on animals that don't have fat reserves to draw on. So how do the chickadees cope? Well, on cold nights, they lower their body temperature from a normal 108 degrees to around 86 degrees. This slows down their rate of metabolism by 25 percent.

This is just another example of design features we see all around us that defy an evolutionary explanation. How did chickadees ever "learn" to lower their body temperature and raise it again?

Of course, God programmed the information into the genes of the chickadees right from the start. They're a testimony to the wonderful God of creation.

Q. *How do the marine iguanas of the Galapagos Islands actually disprove Darwin's theory?*

A. The marine iguanas of the Galapagos Islands are the only lizards to get their food from the sea. They dive to depths of 30 feet to feed on algae and seaweed.

While feeding in the cold waters, the iguanas slow their heart rate and blood flow. This saves oxygen so they can stay submerged for 20 minutes at a time. But the frigid waters present a problem for them maintaining their body temperature around 98.6 degrees Fahrenheit. So, to keep from cooling down too quickly, they're able to restrict the blood flow to the skin, keeping it near the center of the body.

Feeding underwater also presents another problem. How does the iguana stop swallowing all the salt water? Well, it just so happens that it has a special gland that actually removes the salt from the water, allowing the iguana to drink all the salt water it wants to drink.

When you look at all the special features of this unique lizard, it is obvious that these features could not have slowly evolved over millions of years, but had to be in place and working at a single point in time. These traits point to a Creator, and we wonder how Darwin failed to see the clear answers from the Bible.

Q. *Is there really an animal that turns itself inside out as a defense mechanism?*

A. As strange as it sounds, it's true. We even had photos of this in *Creation* magazine!

When a sea cucumber feels threatened, it will actually turn itself inside out, exposing all of its internal organs. The predator then feeds on the organs and swims away. You'd think that this would be the end for the sea cucumber, but it isn't. After all of its organs are gone, the sea cucumber turns right side out and kind of shrinks up into a small blob. Then it begins to regenerate all of the organs that were eaten away by the predator, until it becomes a fully functional sea cucumber once again!

Here's a question for evolutionists: "How many sea cucumbers died trying to learn how to turn inside out and have their organs eaten away and then grow new ones?" This is not a typical response one would expect if evolution were true.

This is one of the many examples we have of behavior that just could not have been a product of evolution. The sea cucumber is a marvelous testimony of God's unique creative powers. As with the rest of the creatures of the sea, the questions of the origin of the sea cucumber are answered in God's Word, beginning with Genesis.

Q. *How are hummingbirds God's tiny miracles?*

A. Well, listen to the following description of just some of the remarkable characteristics of a hummingbird. I'm sure the ONLY word you'll think of is "miracle."

A hummingbird flaps its wings from 50 to 80 times a second. Unlike many birds that have power only on the downbeat, the hummingbird's wings swivel, and this allows power on the upbeat as well.

This requires a VERY high-energy system. One expert said that for a human to keep up the blistering pace of a hummingbird, he would have to consume around 1,300 hamburgers a day and drink 60 quarts of water for cooling purposes. Another expert said that if we were to operate at the energy level of the hummingbird, our hearts would beat 1,260 times a minute and our body temperature would rise to 385 degrees Celsius (725 degrees Fahrenheit) and we'd burst into flames.

You see, for the hummingbird to survive, these and other special features would have to work perfectly, right from the start. Genesis, and NOT evolution, has the answer. God designed it that way from the beginning.

Q. *Are there any examples that contradict the idea that our oceans are billions of years old?*

A. Yes, there certainly are. You know, I often have people ask me questions like, "What about all the dating methods that supposedly show the earth is billions of years old?"

I usually respond by saying, "But what about the large percentage of methods that CONTRADICT the idea that the earth is billions of years old?"

Most people don't realize that many dating methods pose serious problems for those who accept the secular dates. Consider the seafloor.

According to secular scientists, the seafloor is supposed to be three billion years old. Now scientists observe sediment being deposited on the ocean floor. Through various means, and accounting for sediment coming in and being removed, they've been able to measure the net amount of sediment deposited.

Now using this amount and extrapolating backwards, there's only enough sediment to account for 12 million years — and that's assuming there was no sediment to start with!

But Noah's flood would have added LOTS of sediment. In fact, this means the ocean floor could be much younger — as young as 6,000 years — just as the Bible indicates.

Q. *Don't the school textbooks teach that natural selection and evolution go hand in hand?*

A. Sadly, most students in schools and colleges believe that natural selection is basically the same as evolution.

First of all, let me explain that term "natural selection." If two dogs came off Noah's ark after the flood, eventually a large population of dogs would arise. Now, some of these dogs separated from the main group and went off on their own. Because of all the genetic variation that exists in organisms, over a period of time, it's likely that different combinations of genes would result in various groups — even though all came from the original pair of dogs. Because of environmental pressures, such as temperature, different species of dogs (like long-haired and short-haired types) would arise.

Now this has nothing to do with evolution. All that's happening is that because of the tremendous variation in the genes, different arrangements (or species) result.

This is the opposite of evolution, which requires new information to arise. But this fits exactly with the creation account in Genesis. God created distinct kinds of animals and plants to reproduce after their own kind.

Q. *Is the peppered moth in England evidence for evolution?*

A. When I studied about the peppered moth in my biology class at high school, I remember how I was taught there were light and dark forms of this moth, and an in-between shade. BEFORE the Industrial Revolution, birds supposedly saw more dark moths than light ones on the tree trunks and thus ate more dark ones. DURING the Industrial Revolution, because of soot on the trees — the opposite happened. Then the pollution was reduced, and the situation reverted back to the original.

I was taught this was a good example of evolution, but it's only an example of natural selection, which has nothing to do with "molecules-to-man" evolution. So this was never a problem for creationists any way.

Scientists have now revealed that the moths we saw pictured on the trees were laboratory bred — and they were stuck on the trees! These moths don't even live on the tree trunks, but probably in the leaves. In addition, the numbers of each shade of moth caught in traps didn't fit with their theory at all!

It just goes to show that man's word can't always be trusted, but we can ALWAYS trust the Word of God.

Q. *Is there any basis in astronomy for the seven-day week we all accept around the world?*

A. Actually, there isn't. Consider the day. How do we measure the time span of 24 hours? Well, it's based on one complete rotation of the earth.

Now let's think about the year. How do we measure this? Well, the year is based on the earth's revolution around the sun.

Okay, what about the month? Well we all know that the phases of the moon relate to the measurement of the month.

Well, then, where do we get the seven-day week?

What we find is that the seven-day week has no basis in astronomy whatsoever. It comes from the Bible. Its origin is given in Genesis 1, when God created everything in six days and rested for one.

In fact, in Exodus 20:11, God tells the Israelites, as part of the Ten Commandments, that they're to work for six days and rest for one, based on the creation week.

By the way, if God created over millions of years (i.e. if those days were ages as some would like to believe), this would make nonsense of the seven-day week!

Q: *How is the skimmer a problem for the evolutionists?*

A. Skimmers are birds that live along the coast and have a unique way of feeding. These birds fly just above the water with their lower beak skimming the surface. Whenever that beak hits anything in the water, it closes to catch its prey. Now, the friction of the water wears against the lower beak, so in time you'd expect the beak to wear away. But the lower beak of the skimmer continually grows at the same rate that it wears! Actually, skimmers kept in zoos have to have their lower beak trimmed on a regular basis or it will grow out too far past the upper beak. Interestingly, the upper beak of the skimmer doesn't continually grow, but then again it doesn't touch the water anyway and won't wear down.

So, evolutionists have a real problem trying to explain how the lower beak came to continually grow and the upper beak didn't. When we look at the skimmer, we see the wonderful purpose and design of our Creator God. It looks like the skimmer is designed to do what it does do, and what it does do it does do well, doesn't it? I think it does.

Q: *What about another one of those unique Australian animals, the echidna?*

A. It's not just because I'm Australian that I love these creatures from "down under." It's also because they create such problems for evolutionists!

If you were to walk through the Australian countryside and see what looks like a wire brush stuck over an ants' nest, then you have come across an echidna, having a snack. This animal, also known as the spiny anteater, is a scientific puzzle . . . *if* you're an evolutionist.

You see, the echidna, like the platypus, is a mammal. It has milk glands, hair, and a large brain. But, at the same time, it also resembles reptiles and birds. It lays eggs, and its temperature is influenced somewhat by its surroundings!

Now, here's the question for the evolutionist! What on earth could the echidna have evolved *from*? The answer is that evolutionists have no idea! The evidence from the fossil record shows that they haven't changed at all!

It's more logical to conclude that they've never evolved at all. God created them as egg-laying creatures, right from the beginning.

Q. *What is a frozen Siberian salamander?*

A. Well, let me explain — and no, it's not some bizarre gourmet recipe.

In the frozen wastes of Siberia, an amazing salamander is able to survive in suspended animation for years. It can be deep-frozen at temperatures as low as -50 degrees Celsius (-58 degrees Fahrenheit), and then thaw out and run off. It's absolutely amazing!

Scientists aren't sure of the exact mechanism that allows it to do this, but like some other animals, the salamander almost certainly produces "antifreeze" chemicals to replace the water in its tissues and cells. Scientists believe some of these salamanders may have been frozen for thousands of years. Others can't believe this and feel they may have simply fallen through cracks in the ice.

Regardless of how long they've been frozen, the real question for the evolutionists is this: "How did the salamander obtain this remarkable trait?" After all, how many failed to revive until one finally just happened to produce BY CHANCE the right antifreeze for its tissues?

Here's what makes much more sense. The salamanders possessed the created information in their genes to produce this antifreeze, and they were the ones that were able to survive in this icy environment. They were created — the answer's in Genesis!

Q. *What are the special features of the skunk?*

A. When you hear the word "skunk," most people immediately think of odor! But skunks actually have many marvelous design features, and they defy evolution!

Skunks are nocturnal, meaning they're awake at night. They have eyes that allow them to see in the dark. Instead of light being absorbed by the retina as in the human eye, the skunk has a reflective layer that sends the light back through its light sensitive cells. It makes it possible for skunks to see in nearly total darkness!

But there's much more. Skunks have the ability to breed almost any time of the year, but then delay the fertilized egg from implanting in the uterus for up to 200 days. This allows the skunk to wait until spring to give birth when food is plentiful and the youngs' chances for survival are greater.

There's no way that such obvious design features can be accounted for on the basis of chance, evolutionary processes over millions of years.

What a wonderful Creator and provider we have!

Q. *What do ferns have to do with creation, evolution, and the Book of Genesis?*

A. Well, folded ferns actually tell us that the evolutionists' idea of long time periods is in trouble. Let me explain.

Many fern fossil specimens are found associated with coal seams. The frond fossils are believed to be no more than just the leaf litter that fell to the ground in an ancient forest, and somehow were slowly covered and preserved.

But do you know what happens if you take a fern frond and lay it on the ground? It turns brown and rots. If you bury a fern frond, it rots even faster and in a very short time you'll be hard pressed to find any sign of it.

So what should you expect to find from a lot of fern litter that's been buried slowly? A lot of rich soil with very little evidence of fern fronds. Yet we find thousands of fern specimens that have been perfectly preserved. The only explanation is a rapid burial to preserve the fern instead of allowing it to rot away.

What event could account for the rapid burial of ferns all over the earth? The catastrophic judgment of a global flood in Noah's day could easily account for this.

Q. *What is the significance of the famous White Cliffs of Dover in England to the debate over creation and evolution?*

A. The White Cliffs of Dover hug the coastline of southeastern England. These cliffs, which are made primarily of chalk, are eroding at an alarming rate. While we don't have an exact idea how much erosion has occurred at the White Cliffs, we can compare it to what has happened in other parts of England.

For example, a lighthouse near Eastbourne had to be rescued from a cliff's edge. The erosion was more than 70 feet in 165 years, or about 5 inches per year!

Now how does this relate to Genesis and evolution? These rates of erosion contradict the evolutionary belief that landforms are hundreds of millions of years old. If they were that old, the White Cliffs of Dover would have disappeared long ago. Evolution requires millions of years, but rates of erosion argue against it.

The Bible is correct — our earth is on the order of thousands of years old, not millions!

Q. *Did the Grand Canyon form over millions of years by the slow erosion of the Colorado River?*

A. You know, it's so sad that people are still promoting this wrong view of the origin of the Grand Canyon.

I've been to the canyon many times, and it continually frustrates me to have the same park rangers there present an evolutionary view of the canyon's formation.

Now, however, we're noticing that many evolutionary geologists are sort of agreeing with us in that it did NOT take millions of years to be carved!

For a long time, creation scientists have been telling evolutionists that the Grand Canyon does not fit with this idea of millions of years of earth history. They've said that the canyon had to be gouged out quickly by a large quantity of water. Many evolutionists are now conceding this point. They've realized that the Colorado River did not slowly erode the Grand Canyon over millions of years.

Creationists believe the aftermath of Noah's flood had a lot to do with the formation of the Grand Canyon. The answer's in Genesis!

Q. *Why were the "frozen planes" that were discussed in* **Creation** *magazine such a problem?*

A. Actually, it's only a problem for those who believe it takes millions of years for deep layers of ice to accumulate in places like the Arctic and Antarctic.

In 1942 and during World War II, a squadron of P-38 and B-17 planes had to be abandoned after they landed on Greenland's icy coast.

In 1980 searchers began looking for these planes. They thought the planes would be easy to find, but they weren't. Many years and many dollars later, the eight planes were finally found buried 250 feet down in solid ice and three miles from their original location!

The searchers were astounded! You see, evolutionists have conditioned us to believe that it takes thousands of years for just a few feet of ice to form. In fact, on the basis of the way evolutionists have measured ice layers forming, these planes were buried some 2,000 years ago!

You see, it's NOT the facts that speak against the biblical account of a recent creation. It's the mindset of our culture that's been indoctrinated to believe in millions and billions of years. Our answers should come from the Bible.

Q. *What in the world is a giant sea louse?*

A. Well, a giant sea louse has been discovered living on the sea floor. It's under a half a mile of water off Australia's east coast. They called him "Big Boy." You see, this crustacean is over a foot long! Members of this group are usually only about 3/4 of an inch long. Scientists found this giant louse living off the dead creatures that fall to the bottom of the ocean.

Now here's the problem for evolutionists. They've unearthed fossils of this creature supposedly 80 million years old. Now that they've found a live one, they are surprised to discover that this sea louse has not changed in 80 million years!

Of course, creationists insist that the 80 million years never existed.

You know, evolutionists make discoveries all the time of living things that are little or no different to fossils that are claimed to be millions of years old. They haven't changed.

This of course supports the Genesis account of creation — not evolution.

Q. *Some scientists are puzzled about why flying fish are so colorful. Why is this a problem for them?*

A. Well, the reason is because they're evolutionists. What evolutionists call "problems" are really evidences AGAINST their theory.

Let me explain the flying fish. While sailing in tropical seas, one scientist was puzzled about flying fish. Not so much about why they fly, but why they have such colorful wings. These flying fish had yellow, brown, and turquoise wings, and shades ranging from purple to a deep navy blue.

Now, why is this such a problem to the evolutionists? Well, the wings are only extended during flight, so this is the only time the colors can be seen. What confuses them is this: why would evolution give these fish beautifully colored wings that are not used to help them when swimming in the water, or to blend into the colors of coral and so evade capture. Why would they have such colors that are only seen when they fly over the water?

Well, the flying fish didn't evolve. They're a product of the Master Designer, the Creator God of the Bible, who created everything to show His power and majesty.

Q. *Isn't a sea urchin a simple, slimy creature of the sea?*

A. Sea urchins are amazing creatures and marvels of design.

Sea urchins move about very slowly, so slowly in fact, that you'd expect to find various things growing on them, yet you rarely find that happening. Also, because they have long sharp spines, you'd think all sorts of things would catch on them, yet they don't.

If you were to carefully examine a living sea urchin, you'd notice there appear to be two different lengths of its spines. The shorter ones, though, are not spines, but stalks. They have small "pincer-like" structures on the ends. These pincers are constantly busy, picking off the things that catch and try to grow on the outside of the sea urchin.

In other words, these are self-cleaning pincers, and without them most sea urchins would soon die from all the things growing on them.

The question is "How did the sea urchin KNOW that it had to evolve these pincers in order to survive?" They didn't have to know because they were perfectly created to clean themselves from the beginning. Sea urchins were created on day 5 of the Genesis account.

Q.

Why isn't a millipede that produces cyanide killed by its own poison?

A.

Surprisingly, it isn't.

Located within the sides of each segment of this millipede are small chambers that can produce a deadly cyanide liquid when the millipede is threatened. The poison appears as little droplets along its side.

The cyanide is strong enough to make most predators seriously ill if they tried to pick up the millipede. Also, it's strong enough to kill small predators if they tried to eat it. Since the cyanide gives off a peculiar odor, most animals will avoid the millipede altogether.

The millipede has a special kind of mitochondria that helps prevent it from poisoning itself. If evolution were true, then I wonder how many millipedes poisoned themselves before they developed the special features that protected them?

Also, the system that produces the cyanide is extremely complex and would have had to evolve all at the same time, or none of it would have worked. The millipede would be something's dinner.

This millipede had to be specially designed to do what it does do, and what it does do, it does do well! Evolution? No! Creation? Yes!

Q. *Why is the Australian platypus so amazing?*

A. Actually, my favorite evidence for creation is the platypus. People all over the world are intrigued by this fascinating little animal, which, by the way, only lives in Australia. When the platypus was first discovered in 1797 and was sent back to England, the scientists thought it was actually a fraud put together by Chinese taxidermists. Why? Because here we have an animal that has a bill like a duck, a tail like a beaver, hair like a bear, webbed feet like an otter, claws like a reptile or rooster, and poison like a snake. It lays eggs like a turtle, and detects electrical impulses. I'm sure if you found an animal like that you'd think it was a fraud, too!

When you think about it, the platypus is a real enigma to the evolutionists because they believe one animal evolves into another over millions of years. From which animal did the platypus evolve, then? It would have to be just about everything.

Actually, the platypus is my favorite animal because I believe every time an evolutionist looks at the platypus, God smiles. I think He made it just for them. Did the platypus evolve? The answer is found in Genesis. The God of the Bible created all things, including the platypus.

Creation
Evidence
in Space

Q. *Can Christians believe there could be intelligent life elsewhere in the universe?*

A. I remember when a newspaper reporter from *USA Today* called me about evidence of life on Mars.

This reporter asked me, "What would it do to your Christian faith if little green men from Mars came to Earth in spaceships?" I replied that this won't happen, so it's not a valid question.

I explained to this reporter that I've got strong theological reasons why there can't be intelligent life elsewhere in the universe. Now, the Bible is silent concerning the possibility of animal or plant life outside of the earth, though I suspect even this life is unique to earth. You see, the biblical account of creation puts the earth at center stage.

But here's what I believe: Adam's sin brought the judgment of death to the entire universe, and only Adam's descendants can be saved. So there couldn't be another race of intelligent beings that suffer from Adam's sin but have NO opportunity for salvation. This doesn't make sense.

All intelligent beings in this physical universe are descendants of Adam and Eve. That's what the Bible teaches.

Q. *How are exploding stars evidence that the universe is really not that old?*

A. You know, there are many such examples that just defy the idea that the earth and universe are billions of years old as we've been indoctrinated to believe. In fact, over 90 percent of all age-dating methods give dates far younger than evolutionists require.

A supernova, or exploding star, is one of the most brilliant and powerful objects in the universe. Scientists have observed exploding stars, and they predict that one occurs every 25 years in our Milky Way Galaxy.

When a star explodes, it causes a huge expanding dust cloud of debris. Using mathematics, and powerful computers, scientists can calculate how far this dust cloud would travel.

You see, the expanding clouds of debris they see indicate that the universe is only a few thousand years old. Actually, if the universe is billions of years old, scientists have worked out that there are around 7,000 MISSING debris clouds from such explosions!

But these clouds aren't MISSING, and the universe is NOT billions of years old. Our answers from God's Word tell us the truth:

> The heavens declare the glory of God; and the firmament sheweth his handiwork (Ps. 19:1).

And it happened not so long ago!

Q: *How do the moons of Jupiter confirm the Book of Genesis?*

A. One of our resource scientists, Dr. Russell Humphreys, who authored the book *Starlight and Time*, has developed a model of cosmology that's based upon the Bible. Using this foundation, he then used his knowledge of physics to predict the magnetic fields of the Galilean moons of Jupiter — Ganymede, Io, Europa, and Callisto. His predictions were drastically different than those predicted by evolutionary theories.

Now what's so exciting about all this? Well, scientists have now been able to measure the magnetic fields of these moons — and guess what? What they found matched what Russ Humphreys predicted! In other words, the model of cosmology based upon the Bible worked!

Dr. Humphreys predicted that Ganymede would have the largest magnetic field due to its large core size. But Europa's would be small due to its small core size — and *this* is what they found! He also predicted Callisto wouldn't have a magnetic field — and this matched, also.

How many times do we hear evolutionists saying something like, "Well, we have to rewrite our theories since we now have more evidence"?

Scientists like Dr. Humphreys are able to predict answers because they start with the right answers from the Bible.

Q. *We've all been indoctrinated to believe that the stars are millions of years older than the earth. Is this not true?*

A. When you think about it, I'm sure even most Christians tend to think that the stars are older than our globe. But I know FOR SURE that the earth is actually THREE DAYS older than the stars!

Now, how can I say this? Well, the Creator of the universe has told us in His Word that He created the earth on day 1 of the creation week, but the sun, moon, and stars were not made until day 4.

Now, evolutionists believe that the universe began with a big bang billions of years ago, forming most of the stars. They say that millions of years later, the earth formed as a hot molten blob.

But I know for sure that the big-bang theory is wrong. How can I say that? Because the Bible tells me clearly the earth was made three days before the stars, and that it was initially covered with water — it wasn't a hot molten blob.

I can say all this authoritatively, because I have the Word of a witness who saw it all happen — the Creator God of the universe.

Q. *Was there any truth to the newspaper headlines around the world proclaiming that NASA scientists had found evidence that life once existed on Mars?*

A. It seems the secular media and evolutionary scientists, who don't want to believe in a Creator God, are so desperate to find evidence that life is not unique to Earth that they'll make a lot out of very flimsy findings.

There were numerous newspaper reports such as "Life Found on Mars," "Universe Stuffed with Life," and so on.

But what did the evolutionary scientists actually find? They had a potato-sized meteorite found in the Antarctic that they say came from Mars.

Inside this meteorite they found some carbonate globules associated with certain chemicals that can be produced by living things, but these same chemicals CAN ALSO come from non-living sources.

They also supposedly found fossils of small organisms that were 1/100th to 1/1000th the diameter of a human hair. Some scientists said these could be mud cracks or the result of many other possible causes.

Other scientists who examined the same rock said there was NO evidence of life.

Sadly, man will go to great lengths to avoid the obvious answer from Genesis: God created life!

Q: *What are evolutionists now saying about their big-bang theory of the origin of the universe?*

A. A popular and expensive documentary appeared in my homeland of Australia recently. It portrayed the big bang as a fact. Frankly, there are evolutionary scientists who don't even accept it, not just the creationists.

Answers in Genesis rejects the big bang not only because it's bad science, but most importantly because the Bible teaches against it. You see, the Bible says that the earth was created before the sun; but the big bang says that the sun was created before the earth — a direct conflict!

In this documentary, called *Universe*, the question of extraterrestrial life was also brought up. The narrator confidently declared that there IS intelligent life in outer space. And here's why he said we haven't found them yet: "So far, the aliens have been coy!" And that's his BEST evidence for extraterrestrial, intelligent life? They're simply playing hard-to-get?

The creation account in the Bible is at least logical when it comes to the question of the origins of life and the universe. Psalm 19:1 says that the heavens declare the glory of God; they certainly don't show any evidence of being created by a big-bang explosion!

Q: *How on earth could bacteria have anything to do with messages from space?*

A. Nearly 30 years ago, one of the discoverers of the molecule of heredity, DNA, recognized that this highly complex information system couldn't arise by chance processes. He therefore came up with the idea that some intelligent beings elsewhere in the universe sent bacterial spores to "seed" life on earth.

He proposed that the spores would be like those of *Bacillus subtilis,* which are extremely resistant to radiation and drying out. Then someone else suggested that if this was true, then this intelligence may have also put encoded messages in the DNA, telling us about our origins!

Well, researchers have now decoded the four million letters of the genetic code of this bacterium, equivalent to over one thousand pages of typed material. And they found NO message from outer space!

If they really want a message that originated beyond our planet about how life started, all they have to do is open the Bible. They'll find a message already sent to us from the infinite intelligence about how life originated. What's more, this message in Genesis is not hidden in code, but is there for all to read and understand!

Q. *Why is there such an emphasis today on people looking for aliens from space?*

A. This is certainly the subject of many popular magazines and blockbuster movies. But what are some of the motives behind this?

One renowned science fiction writer suggests that extraterrestrials may be continuously broadcasting an easily decoded "Encyclopedia Galactica" which will answer the basic questions of life. NASA has often justified its search for extraterrestrial life as a quest for answers to the great questions of life on earth: What are we doing here? Where are we going?

We *do* need answers to life's questions. But we don't need to wait for such an "Encyclopedia Galactica" from outer-space aliens, because God has already given us what we could call an "Encyclopedia Biblica" right here on earth! In other words, the Bible, God's Word, DOES contain the answers to questions that philosophers and scientists have been asking for centuries. And it all starts with Genesis!

The motives behind this search for aliens is that most scientists don't want to believe Genesis, because that would mean they're sinners in need of salvation.

Creation
vs.
Evolution

Q. *I know that evolutionists constantly attack creationists, but I understand that there is even some infighting going on in evolution circles, right?*

A. Yes, there is. While evolutionists and creationists have been debating for 150 years, listeners might be surprised to learn that evolutionists are arguing a lot with each other. In the long run, they're helping show that creation is true.

There are two major groups of evolutionists. They're often identified as those who follow Stephen J. Gould of Harvard University or those who follow Richard Dawkins of Oxford University in England. Followers of Dawkins say that "evolution occurred slowly and gradually," but followers of Gould say that evolution occurred in spurts, with rapid evolution of animals. It once got so heated between the two factions that one of Dr. Gould's colleagues at Harvard was drenched with water during a debate over these two views of evolution.

These two groups are actually helping the creationists. You see, their "house divided" only shows that the fossil record is not a help to evolution. Fossils actually show that animals do not change into other animals. After all, the Bible records that all animals reproduce after their kind.

Q. *Is it possible that a practicing scientist can also be a creationist?*

A. Evolutionists often claim that if you believe in creation, you can't be a true scientist. However, I've met a number of real scientists who ARE creationists. One such scientist is Dr. Gary Parker, who has spoken with me at some of our seminars. He has a very distinguished science background.

We need to also understand that many of the most famous scientists who ever lived were creationists. For instance, think about names like Michael Faraday, James Clerk Maxwell, Isaac Newton, Johannes Kepler . . . and the list goes on. These were some of the most famous scientists who ever lived, and they believed Genesis.

I had the opportunity to speak to a number of scientists at the Goddard Space Center near Baltimore. It excited me to see the number of scientists (*real* scientists who were involved in building the space shuttle and repairing the Hubble Telescope) who told me they believed that Genesis is accurate. They did not accept evolution. There are probably thousands of scientists like this throughout the world — practicing scientists who believe in creation.

What should scientists believe about where we came from? God created all things.

Q. *Many Christians believe that Darwin rejected his idea of evolution on his deathbed. Is that true?*

A. It's true that Darwin rejected a *belief system* at the time of his death, but it WASN'T his evolutionary belief system. It was the truth of God's word that Darwin turned his back on.

Many Christians believe that Darwin changed his mind about evolution just before he died. A tract written by a certain Lady Hope has been widely distributed; she supposedly had such a conversation with Darwin while he was dying.

But all investigation has shown that this tract has no factual basis. Actually, Darwin made statements shortly before he died which indicated he didn't believe there'd been ANY revelation from God. He also said that the Old Testament was to be no more trusted than the sacred books of the Hindus. Actually, Darwin admitted that the more he believed evolution, the more he rejected God.

This should be a solemn warning for the Church. The more Christians believe in evolution, the more they'll reject God's Word. Let's be careful.

Q. *Don't evolutionists have different evidence than the creationists?*

A. When I've had the opportunity to debate an evolutionist on a radio program, one of the first things I say is that I actually agree with all the evidence an evolutionist has.

I also say to him or her that there's nothing he or she observes in this world that I disagree with.

I go on to explain that in reality, creationists and evolutionists have all the same evidence: we have the same earth, same universe, same fossils, same animals and plants — all the evidence is the same. You see, the battle between creation and evolution is not about the evidence; it's about how one INTERPRETS the evidence in relation to the past.

The point I make is that as human beings, in the present, observing this world, everything we see is the same. When we're trying to understand where everything came from, however, then we have to step back into history, but we don't have the past. For Christians we have a revelation (the Bible) that tells us the history of the past, which makes sense of the evidence in the present. Evolutionists have beliefs about the past that don't ultimately make sense of the evidence of the present.

The Bible's true, from its very first verse!

Q. *Has anyone ever tried to update Darwin's classic book,* **The Origin of the Species,** *using the supposed latest evidences for evolution?*

A. Actually, Dr. Steve Jones from London University (someone I debated on British TV) has done just that. He wrote a book entitled *Almost Like a Whale*. This book follows through the actual chapter headings in Darwin's book. It's claimed that this is the updated version of Darwin's *Origin of the Species*.

I must admit, the more of the book I read, the more I shook my head in utter amazement. You see, I realized that evolutionists today really have nothing new to add to Darwin. Yes, their arguments are a bit more sophisticated and they use some different examples. But, the basic thrust of the book is that speciation (changes we observe within a "kind of animal") happens all around us.

Creationists of course have no problem with speciation. The changes that occur in populations of birds, such as finches or crows, only involve the genetic material that was already present.

You see, for "molecules-to-man" evolution to occur, a process is required that provides brand new information into the genes. Nowhere in the book was such an example documented. There is no evidence for such a process.

Q. *How can the average Christian know how to deal with educated evolutionists?*

A. I've found that many Christians think they can't say much about creation or oppose evolution because they're not scientists. But the good news is that you really don't have to be an expert to refute evolution and defend the Book of Genesis. The main arguments are quite simple. Yes, you'll need to do some reading, but you don't have to be intimidated by even a research scientist who knows the evidence for evolution!

For instance, one of the questions God asked Job was, "Where were you when I laid the foundations of the earth?" In other words, God really asked Job, "Were you there?" This is one of the questions I teach children to think about whenever someone says they believe in "millions of years."

A friend of mine told me of his conversation with an evolutionary geologist. This evolutionist went on and on about the layers of rocks and their millions of years. Finally, my friend just said to the man, "Were you there?" The geologist was dumb-founded.

The true answers to evolution are quite simple, so don't be afraid to defend the Book of Genesis.

Q: *Is the topic of origins — creation versus evolution — really an important one in talking with our non-Christian friends?*

A. Actually, I think it's absolutely important to understand that evolution is one of the biggest stumbling blocks today to the gospel of Jesus Christ.

When I visited Edinburgh, Scotland, a number of university students came up after I'd given a lecture on creation and said, "We suddenly realized something tonight. You see, when we're trying to witness to non-Christians at the university, they always bring up the same two questions."

I stopped them and said: "I can tell you what those two questions are: creation/evolution and death and suffering."

"Yes," they said surprisingly, "they're the two that come up over and over again." They added: "But we've been told by our churches to ignore those questions and just tell them about Jesus dying for their sins on the Cross. What you're telling us is that we need to deal with those questions to show that we CAN give answers for what we believe. To show them that evolution is NOT a proven fact, so that they now will listen when we talk about the gospel message."

And I said, "That's exactly what we need to be doing."

THAT'S how we should witness effectively to non-Christians!

Q: *In England there was an appeal for millions of dollars to be raised to restore Charles Darwin's house. What were your thoughts?*

A. There's a very important lesson for us all to learn about Charles Darwin's home being threatened by dereliction.

The roof had fallen in on Darwin's lab; the main house had a leaky roof; the walls of the study were being attacked by damp and woodworm. Without a great deal of effort, this home would eventually become a total ruin.

You know, there's a touch of irony to all of this. Darwin popularized the idea to millions and millions of people that everything has made itself, and that nature has, on a grand scale, organized matter from simple to complex . . . from chaos to cosmos!

But in reality, virtually every single scientific observation confirms that the very OPPOSITE is true. What we observe is that, because of the Curse as a result of sin, everything that's left to itself tends to run down — just like Darwin's house!

Darwin's house won't rebuild itself. It will require a lot of intelligence and energy to improve it.

Likewise, the infinite Creator God created the first man from dust. Darwin's decaying home should be a lesson to trust Genesis!

Q. *In an article in our* Creation *magazine, you reported about your trip to England to visit Charles Darwin's grave. Tell us about it.*

A. I usually visit England at least once a year. Even though there are some good churches, there's not much biblical Christianity left in public life. And this was once a nation where most people believed in the Creator God.

What's happened? Let me share my experience at Westminster Abbey, the big church in London. Here many famous people are buried: kings and queens, and a number of famous scientists like Sir Isaac Newton, who was a believer in the Bible. I also found out that another very famous person is buried there — Charles Darwin!

Darwin is actually buried in the floor of the church! When I found his grave there, it suddenly struck me what had happened to the Church in England. You see, the man who popularized the philosophy of evolution, which destroys the foundation of the Church, was honored by the Church and buried in the FOUNDATION of the church.

The Church honored Darwin instead of honoring God's Word. The Church today needs to return to the proper foundation that God is Creator.

Q. *Many evolutionists admit that there are problems with the theory of evolution, yet they're unwilling to even consider creation as a possibility. Is there a reason why?*

A. There sure is!

After Adam had sinned, what was Adam and Eve's first response to God as He approached them in the Garden of Eden? Well, they hid.

Why? Because they felt guilty in His presence. They were ashamed of themselves in the presence of a perfect and holy God.

Man has been trying to hide from God ever since.

When you think about it, evolution is a very effective way to hide from the Creator. Evolution teaches people there's no God, so if they chose to believe this, then they don't have to face Him. By not facing God in their unbelief, they're hiding from Him, just as Adam and Eve tried to do in the Garden.

This is one of the reasons why humanists don't even want the possibility of creation permitted in public schools. To allow this, is to open the door to showing these young people that they need to face up to the God against whom they have sinned and have been hiding from.

Evolution's Agenda

Q: *When we visit museums, we see many professionally produced displays. They're so well done that we feel we can trust everything we see. Should we, though?*

A. Actually, we have to be VERY careful about what we view in museums. When we see those displays illustrating man's evolution (i.e., showing beings that are supposedly half-ape and half-man), we need to realize that the scientists didn't dig up the flesh and hair; they actually used a lot of artistic license to put flesh and hair on the pieces of bones they found.

In many instances, scientists have only found a few of the bones of the skeleton anyway, but usually you're not told what was really found.

Also, keep in mind that we now know of many mistakes that scientists have made that were once presented as truth. For instance, Neanderthal man was once displayed as our apeish ancestor. But scientists found out their original description of Neanderthal man was wrong. Today he's pictured as upright and human, just like you and me, not a brute!

We can't always trust what we see in museums, but we can certainly ALWAYS trust what we read in the Bible.

Q. *What does "living like animals" have to do with a paradox in society?*

A. Through our secular education system, students are taught they're just animals that have evolved from other animals. Therefore, animal instincts and behavior from their primitive ancestors have been passed down to them. Is it any wonder, then, that we see so many young people today living like animals and trying to satisfy their animal lusts for sex, power, and blood?

Now a society must remain consistent with its own teachings. If it teaches people that they're just animals, then they're accountable to no one but themselves, so why shouldn't they do whatever they want to?

But — and here's the paradox — the very same evolutionary society that tells them they're animals punishes them for being consistent when they act like animals by stealing, killing, and so on.

The inconsistency is so obvious, and the more people realize this, the more they'll rebel against the rules of the culture.

Today's society is trying to govern and rule based upon a world view that has no basis with which to govern and rule!

But Genesis teaches that there's a Creator God to whom we're accountable, and whose laws we're obligated to obey.

Q. *Do you think most of the secular media sensationalizes just about anything they think will undermine Christianity?*

A. I sure do! Remember the hype surrounding the supposed finding of evidence of life in a meteorite from Mars?

This received front-page headlines! Even though the scientists themselves warned people to be cautious about the evidence, the media made a tremendous splash across the world, making outlandish statements.

I was flooded with calls from reporters who saw this as an opportunity to slam Christians and particularly creationists.

But what most people miss is the fact that two groups of scientists who investigated the SAME meteorite released papers in respectable journals stating there was NO evidence of life in this meteorite. One such report was printed way back on page 16 of our local newspaper.

A similar thing happened a few years ago. Newspapers printed front-page stories that scientists had found amino acids on a meteorite indicating that life came from outer space. But a few months later, a small item appeared in the back of the newspaper stating that a scientist found the amino acids came from contamination from (are you ready?) human dandruff!

Beware of those in the secular media who try to suppress the truths of Genesis.

Q. *Can America still be called a great nation?*

A. Frankly, it's no longer the Christian country it used to be. You'd have to say that it's really a post-Christian nation. As you observe the growing humanist philosophy in the increasing abortion, homosexual behavior, pornography, and violence — as well as the growing anti-Christian sentiment — you have to conclude that something terrible has happened to this nation.

What's happened can be described as a "culture shift." Generations ago, American society was based on the Bible. Thus, people had a Christian morality, by and large. But the Bible is no longer the foundation it used to be. Increasingly, it's being replaced by an evolutionary foundation. Thus, people are being taught that man is just animal, that the Bible is not true; therefore, people can decide truth for themselves.

As a result of this change, the American culture has changed from a Christian one to a secular one. People have no understanding of sin or Christian morality anymore. That's why we need to get people back to the authority of the Word of God, beginning with Genesis.

Q. *Is America tolerant to Christians?*

A. Here in America, there's a group called "People for the American Way." It promotes itself as "open minded" and in favor of freedom of expression. That's why "American Way" is in its name. For all its claims to be tolerant, it's engaged in a long campaign of censoring Christianity. Now they are directing their efforts at creationists. In a report that came out, they attacked our Answers in Genesis ministry.

By the way, their paper was filled with errors. In fact, the very first sentence in the report contained a gross error when it declared that Kansas "removed" evolution from the state curriculum. No such thing ever happened.

It's curious that the People for the American Way attacked our ministry for being so dogmatic. At the same time, they dogmatically insist that our views are wrong and shouldn't be heard in the classrooms.

It appears that secular humanists are now even more devoted to censoring those who hold different views. As an organization that calls itself a "civil rights group," People for the American Way is betraying its name!

Q. *Do you blame abortion and lawlessness on evolution as the liberal group "People for the American Way" recently claimed?*

A. No, of course I don't. In fact, the root cause of social problems is sin, the rebellion against God's Word. But in people's minds today, what really justifies this rebellion against God's Word? If we're honest, it's evolution.

Because people have been taught that man evolved from ape-like creatures, and that the Bible's account of origins in Genesis can't be accepted, they believe they're not responsible to anyone but themselves. This means that ultimately they can do whatever they want.

Evolution so permeates our society that more and more people believe that the Bible's not true. There-fore, they don't have to be obedient to God's Word. And the more people believe they're just animals in the fight for survival, then why shouldn't they justify homosexual behavior or abortion?

Evolutionists themselves admit this connection with evolution, abortion, and homosexuality. In the magazine *Scientific American*, an author admitted that social issues like abortion and homosexuality are in "Darwin's beat."

The more people believe in evolution and reject the Bible, the more we're going to see an increase in anti-God behavior.

Q. *Was someone deliberately killed in a hospital simply because the bed was needed?*

A. That's exactly what I'm saying. A Dutch study about euthanasia in Holland found that in a single year, there were more than 2,700 euthanasia deaths. These were people who were deliberately killed by a doctor. Fifty percent of them were NOT even given a choice.

One elderly lady didn't want to be admitted to the hospital because she thought the doctors would put her away. Her own doctor assured her he wouldn't do that. But while he was away, someone else killed her because they needed her bed for another patient.

There's no doubt that euthanasia, or patient killing, is one of the most critical issues ever to face society.

Actually, it's a logical outcome of years of intense indoctrination in evolution. You see, when people believe they're just evolved animals, then killing a human is no different than putting away a dog or cat. From an evolutionary perspective, it makes sense to rid the world of the old, sick, or deformed. Who decides right or wrong? We do!

This is why Christians need to stand against this evil of evolution and teach the answers from the Bible: all humans are very special. We're made in the image of God.

Q. *If evolution is "survival of the fittest," why would evolutionists even bother to care for others?*

A. You know, that's an important question. You see, if we're just a part of this struggle for survival — animals ripping each other apart — and as the poet said, "nature red (with blood) in tooth and in claw," then why WOULD we care for others, particularly the old and sick?

It's interesting to note that it was really the Christians who started our modern hospitals, orphanages, and schools, to care for others. That's because our God is a God who loves and cares.

Recently, a doctor from Europe (which is just saturated in evolutionary humanism) related what happened when he took his father to the hospital. The doctors prescribed morphine. But when this man looked at the prescription, he realized, as a doctor himself, that it was a lethal dose! He explained to us that many old people don't want to go to the hospital in these places any more because they may receive a lethal injection!

This practice is sure to spread if people don't return to God's Word, beginning with Genesis.

Q. *Isn't evolution much more than the idea of millions of years, fossil men, and so on?*

A. In a very broad sense, evolution is really a whole philosophy of life that teaches that man, by himself, can determine truth.

Most people, when they consider evolution, think about millions of years of earth history, or transitional forms, ape-men, or life evolving from chemicals. But this is just a part of what evolution is all about.

You see, people who don't accept the authority of God's Word have to find an explanation about where the universe and life came from.

Because they reject the Word of God, they're saying, in effect, that man by himself can determine truth. On the other hand, Christians should recognize that man can't find truth by himself. We must start with the One who is truth, who has given us all the answers we need, to come to right conclusions.

Sadly, Christians who accept evolution are really saying that man can come to truth by himself, and then fallible man can reinterpret God's Word accordingly. Christians need to realize that evolution is an anti-God religion. It's not the answer!

Q. *What do evolutionists give as the BEST possible evidence for "molecules to man" evolution?*

A. I once participated in a kind of debate with evolutionists on BBC Television when I was in Great Britain. One of my opponents was a leading evolutionary scientist, Dr. Steve Jones, from London University.

During the debate I said, "I'd like to ask the scientists a question. If I want to convince the public that evolution is true, instead of just generalizing the fossil record, what's something that you think is absolutely convincing that evolution is true?"

Dr. Jones replied, "Here's my example. It's come up in the last 10 years. Two species of salmon in American lakes. . . . And in the last 20 years they've split into two forms, one big, one small, one goes to the sea, one stays at home. That's the origin of species seen in our own lifetime."

I responded, "That's speciation, but that's not evolution in the molecules-to-man sense. They're *still* salmon."

Then Dr. Jones said: "What is evolution if it isn't? What was Darwin's book called? It was called *The Origin of Species.*"

I was amazed, but not really surprised. The evidence he gave of speciation has **NOTHING** to do with molecules-to-man evolution, but everything to do with changes within the biblical "kind."

Q. *This may seem like a silly question, but what is the difference between cats and children?*

A. Actually, the difference depends upon the world view you have!

People who accept evolution are more inclined to believe that there's not much difference between cats and children. They believe they're all just animals anyway. Sadly, this has had an enormous influence on the way people view abortion.

If evolution's true, and if man's just an animal, then what's in a mother's womb is just an animal. If you didn't want the child developing in its mother's womb, you'd get rid of it just as you would get rid of spare cats.

What's so sad in our cultures today is that people will spend several days and a lot of money trying to find a home for a cat, or they'll protest against animal research and demand animal rights. But these same people think nothing of having an abortion to get rid of an unwanted child.

Because of intense evolutionary indoctrination, people have abandoned the absolutes of God's Word. Since our society has by and large turned from the truths of Scripture, then there are no absolutes. All becomes relative, and humans aren't special any way. The answer is to return to the absolute authority of the Word of God.

Q. *Who are "Christian Humanists"? Isn't this a contradiction in terms?*

A. Have you noticed that when it comes to moral issues, so many of our leaders in government and education seem to side with the humanists?

Not only do they side with them, but you'll find that many of our leaders attend church and claim to be Christians. Why do leaders in the Church often side with the humanists on moral issues such as homosexual behavior, abortion, and so on?

The main reason, I believe, is because the Church, by and large, has accepted evolutionary ideas. Now, that may be surprising, but think about it. People have been taught that God's Word, and particularly the Book of Genesis must be reinterpreted on the basis of man's evolutionary ideas. They've been trained to think that their opinions are a higher authority than God's Word. As a result, they do not use God's Word as the foundation for their thinking.

Also, most of these people have been trained in a public education system that's anti-God. They think in terms of a secular world view.

In a real sense, we could say that the Church is producing humanistic-thinking Christians (thus my term "Christian Humanists"). The Church needs to find its answers in God's Word, beginning with Genesis, and abandon compromise.

Q. *It's very difficult to imagine anyone supporting the violence of abortion. Yet, "choice" seems to be the word "of choice" in society today. What has helped cause this?*

A. Well, God allows us to make choices. But at the same time, He tells us what moral choices He expects us to make. And He also tells us the price we'll pay for our disobedience.

The Bible clearly tells us that ever since the Fall, people have been in rebellion against the Creator. We'd much rather justify our own actions than to do what God has said is right.

A friend in Arizona shared an article with me on the hypocrisy of the abortion rights movement. A 15-year-old girl was arrested for killing her newborn baby, yet if she had aborted her child, she would have been just fine according to the law.

Really, there's no difference between being just out of the womb, and being inside only moments before!

Actually, almost all biologists, Christians or not, will tell you that life begins at conception. More importantly, the Bible reveals that God created humans in His image, and that murder is sin. Abortion may be legal right now, but it violates God's moral law.

Evolution
in
Education

Q. *In what ways do you say school textbooks are outdated?*

A. As a former public school science teacher myself, I've noticed a pattern in public school and college textbooks over the years.

Publishers try to keep the textbooks updated with the latest findings and scientific advances in MOST areas — except, however, for the sections dealing with evolution.

I gathered textbooks from school districts in different states in America and carefully went through the chapters that dealt with evolution. I found that many of the arguments for evolution that had been thrown out years ago by the scientific establishment were still being presented dogmatically in these texts.

Arguments such as embryonic recapitulation (it was discredited over 50 years ago), the horse evolution series (this was being greatly modified in the 1970s), vestigial organs like the appendix supposedly having no function (this was refuted many years ago) were all there, and the list goes on.

Why do textbooks still contain these outdated arguments? It's difficult to say for sure, but I suspect it's because the authors so want students to believe in evolution that they're hesitant to remove these seemingly powerful but discredited arguments.

Q. *How can you say that public schools are churches?*

A. They are really churches of humanism. You see, secular humanists view public schools as important for promoting their ideas. Actually, they're quite open about the fact that they've used the public school system to indoctrinate our children in humanism.

A few years ago, an article appeared in a magazine called *The American Humanist*. The author claimed that the battle for mankind's future would be waged — and won — in the public school classroom. Teachers would be converting children to the religion of humanism.

One of the ways in which they accomplish this is by teaching evolution as fact throughout the public school education system. Today millions of children are being indoctrinated, almost daily, in the belief that they're just animals, and that there's no God and that the Bible isn't true.

You know, a student can be well educated, but if he or she worships the creature, as evolution teaches, not the Creator, then they'll be lost for eternity. All their education amounts to nothing if they've not accepted Jesus Christ, the Creator, as Lord and Savior.

Q. *I heard that you were restricted as to what you could tell a Christian club at a public school. Yet a teacher was allowed to ridicule the Bible all he wanted to in class. Tell us about it!*

A. I was asked to speak at a Christian club at a high school in Canada. When I arrived I was ushered into the supervising teacher's office before the meeting. I was warned not to offend anyone and only to speak on things that we all agreed on.

Later that night, one of the students told me that his teacher spent the next class period of 45 minutes degrading everything that I'd said.

What struck me was that I, as a Christian, was told what I could and could not say. But someone who was NOT a Christian was allowed to say whatever he wanted to against Christianity.

Sadly, the same is true in public schools in the United States. Teachers can say anything they want against the Bible, but Christians are denied the right to proclaim the truths of the Bible.

Our freedoms are rapidly decreasing, while the freedoms to slander the Creator God are upheld. Christians need to take a stand!

Q. *Many Christian teachers in public school systems look on themselves as missionaries in a pagan system. How can they effectively teach creation?*

A. It's very difficult for Christian teachers in this setting. In America, the humanists have been successful in virtually outlawing the Bible and its teachings.

But as a former public school teacher myself, I believe that Christian teachers can effectively teach against evolution without even mentioning the Bible or creation. They can simply teach students HOW TO THINK.

You see, I found that most science classes only instruct the students in WHAT to think, not HOW to think. When you teach students the right way to think, they'll easily see that evolution isn't science, but just a belief.

I made sure my students understood what science is, but also what it isn't. I taught them that real science involved using the five senses in the present to build computers, space shuttles, and so on. But, when you come to origins, you've just stepped outside this sort of science. You're now dealing with the beliefs of scientists who were not there.

I found that students quickly caught on, and then asked questions like, "Well, how CAN we know where we came from?" What a great opening to give them the answer — God created!

Q: *Has evolutionary indoctrination in schools affected students in any way?*

A. Much more than most people realize.

When I lived in California a few years ago, I read a report in a local newspaper that described the results of a survey taken of public school students. Those who conducted this survey were absolutely astonished to find that one in four students had contemplated, or were contemplating, suicide! They went on to write that they didn't understand why there was this sense of purposelessness and hopelessness in public school students.

And you know, suicide is one of the biggest causes of teenage death today. In my country of Australia, it was recently stated in the newspapers that suicide had become the number one cause of teenage death.

Why is this happening? I think it's simple. You take generations of young people and teach them they came from slime, they don't know why they're here or where they're going, they just evolved by chance, and they're just animals. Then why shouldn't they want to end it all? After all, there's absolutely no purpose and meaning in life.

How can we change their attitude? We need to teach that God created them, and that there is purpose in life.

Q. *Do you think that children — even from Christian homes — should be taught evolution?*

A. My answer is a very definite YES! Let me explain!

Sadly, I've had some Christian parents tell me that their children were only going to learn about creation and hear nothing about evolution. But they're wrong.

You see, my children know more about evolution than most evolutionists. We've nothing to be worried about if we teach our children the TRUTH about evolution. In fact, it's imperative that they learn it.

Children need to be taught that evolution has no basis in science, that there are no facts that support it, and that it's actually an evil philosophy. In fact, the men who popularized evolution wanted to stop people from believing the God of creation. You know, the more our children know about evolution, the more they'll see that it has no basis in truth whatsoever!

We must obey the Scriptures and teach our children to distinguish good from evil, as the Book of Hebrews tells us. And to do this, we must train them in the truth of creation and teach them the fallacy of evolution.

Q. *What is the National Academy of Sciences, and what is its agenda?*

A. The National Academy of Sciences is a private body, but with a mandate granted by the U.S. Congress, to advise the federal government on scientific matters.

This organization produced a 140-page book to be sent to the public school system, its teachers, and school boards across America. The purpose of the book is to instruct educators to teach evolution and ONLY evolution in the science classroom.

Throughout the book, teachers are told to teach evolution as FACT, and to tell students that NO scientist rejects evolution.

As you read through this book, you also find that the authors vehemently go against anyone who takes the Book of Genesis literally or believes the Bible to be the inerrant Word of God.

Why did they publish this book? I believe it's because these evolutionists recognize that the creation movement has reached thousands of people with the truths of Genesis. The evolutionists can't combat this teaching with facts. So what's their strategy? They're pushing teachers to ensure students are more heavily indoctrinated in evolution and that they never hear about creation.

Evolutionary Infiltration in the Church

Q: *Are evolutionists aggressive in pushing their ideas on the world?*

A. Very definitely! They're desperate to try to convince the world that their anti-God religion is true. Consider some of these emotional press reports just a few years ago: NASA announced it had supposedly found evidence of life on Mars, which according to them meant life on Earth was not special. Then we were told scientists had found a feathered dinosaur in China "proving" dinosaurs evolved into birds.

Evolutionists also said they found evidence that the dinosaurs were wiped out by an asteroid that hit the earth 65 million years ago. Some scientists said that the cloning of "Dolly," the sheep, and a couple of monkeys would lead to evidence for evolution.

The Pope even made a statement that evolution was "more than a hypothesis"!

Evolutionary ideas are being pushed on the public around the world. But you know what's true for sure? Claim after claim made by the evolutionists is being rejected as scientists look more carefully at the evidence. There's NO life on Mars. There were NO feathers on the dinosaur. Cloning has absolutely nothing to do with evolution. We've reported on all of these finds in our *Creation* magazine.

NOTHING has been or ever will be found to contradict the Bible.

Q. *Are you being divisive when you take a very strong stand concerning such things as the six literal days of creation, a young earth, and the global flood?*

A. At a recent seminar, a young woman told me that her pastor refuses to take a stand on these issues. She said it would create too much division. The pastor thought it would offend some of the academics in his church.

I explained to this woman that just because something is divisive, doesn't mean it's wrong. We're told in the Bible that there's division because of what Jesus taught! In fact, in a world where "men love darkness rather than light," there'll be division when Scripture shines on this dark world. Really, if you're not causing division (for the right reasons), you may not be teaching the truth of Scripture!

I also reminded this woman that if her pastor doesn't discuss the first chapters of Genesis, he'll also have to avoid much of Paul's teachings in the New Testament. Many passages are dependent on a literal Genesis!

Christians should take a stand on six literal days, a young earth, and global flood even if it causes division. Either God means what He says, or we may as well not believe any of the Bible.

Q. *Is it true that many of the world's leading atheists and evolutionists once attended church?*

A. Yes, I've read testimonies from atheists who say that they were brought up in a Bible-believing, conservative Christian home. We might then ask the question, "What happened to them?" It's interesting to note that many of them say that it was because of the teaching of evolution that they rejected Christianity, and then turned to atheism.

A prominent evolutionist at Harvard has written that he even made a profession of faith in Christ while growing up in one of America's southern states.

Regrettably, the Church has not defended the Book of Genesis to counteract evolutionary teaching. This is why so many people who have been brought up in the Church are now rejecting Christianity. These people saw the hypocrisy of Church leaders stating that the Bible is God's Word, and yet they didn't believe the first chapters of its first book.

You know, I think many churches and Christian colleges would be shocked if they discovered where each person who sat under their compromising teaching had ended up today.

The Bible teaches clearly that compromise destroys! We need to return to the authority of God's Word and its answers.

Q. *I hear many people calling for a revival in our nations, but why do you say we need a new reformation?*

A. When you think carefully about it, the great revivals of the past occurred when people understood they were sinners and that they needed to repent before a Holy God. In other words, people had a fear and reverence for God and His Word.

When you look at nations today like England, in which great revivals occurred generations ago, there's very little vestige of Christianity left in public life. The Church, by and large, is dead, with only pockets of small Bible-believing churches struggling to make an impact on what's now a very pagan culture.

Sadly, in such nations, most of the churches have compromised the Word of God, particularly in Genesis. Most of the church leaders believe in evolution and/or billions of years. They don't — and can't — preach authoritatively from the Word of God.

If we want to see revivals again in nations, I believe there has to be a new reformation in the churches first, with God's people returning to God's Word and accepting it as authoritative. This must begin with the Church repenting of compromise and believing God's Word, beginning with Genesis.

Q. *Surely Church leaders have a high view of the Bible, don't they?*

A. Please don't get me wrong. There are many church leaders, of course, who have a very high opinion of Scripture, as we all ought to have. But sadly, there's an increasing number of Christian leaders who, I believe, have a very LOW view of God's Word.

While in England, I came across Sunday school material produced by a major Christian organization. Many conservative, evangelical churches use it. One series of lessons covered the topic of origins.

I was dismayed when the text declared that people need to believe in billions of years and evolution. But I was even *more* shocked when I read that the apostle Paul didn't understand science back in his time as we understand it today. Therefore, they concluded, what Paul wrote was not meant to answer questions about man's origins for today's world!

What a low view of Scripture! They're looking on Paul's writings as the writings of a fallible human. But every word in the Bible was written under the inspiration of the Holy Spirit — it's the Word of God who knows everything!

Q. *Is evolution only about life evolving?*

A. Evolution actually involves much more than life arising from non-life by natural means. Evolution really does away with God, and thus allows people to explain their existence without any supernatural being involved.

In fact, evolution is a whole philosophy of life that teaches that man by himself can determine truth — that there's no God. In other words, they believe that life can be explained solely on the basis of what they see acting around them today. In essence, this is their religion!

Part of the evolutionist's religion is that energy from the sun, acting on a primeval soup millions of years ago, caused the first life forms to emerge. Thus, they believe that the sun really gave birth to living things. They're really giving glory to the sun's energy for life.

Down through the ages, culture after culture has worshiped the sun. If you recall, the Israelites were warned not to worship the sun as did the pagan nations around them.

Scientists may claim that evolution has nothing to do with religion, but it's their religion to worship creation instead of the God who created the sun and all life.

Q. *What have you discovered about Satanism and evolution?*

A. Well, I've always said that evolution is an anti-God religion, and that the more people believe it and act consistently, the more anti-God they'll become.

Anton LaVey wrote the Satanic Bible and founded the Church of Satan. Now the truth is that this man's anti-God actions were *directly* influenced by his belief in evolution.

Among the passages in the Satanic Bible, LaVey wrote verses such as this one: "It is this unshakable will to live that, if man were not so 'highly evolved,' would also give him the fighting spirit he needs to stay alive." (Or, "If man were not dulled through this stifling evolutionary development. . . .")

There are a number of other passages from the Satanic Bible that deal with evolution — even in the book's introduction. There's no doubt that LaVay was directly influenced by Darwinian evolution when he established the Church of Satan, an anti-God religion!

This is why it's SO important for us to spread the TRUTH about Genesis. We must oppose the anti-God religion of evolution that pervades our education systems worldwide.

---

1. Anton La Vey, *Satanic Bible* (New York, NY: Avon Books, 1969), p. 91.

Q. *Are there quotations from some of the early church fathers many centuries ago showing that they didn't necessarily believe in six literal days of creation? Now shouldn't we take note of the words of these great men?*

A. When I was at a public meeting in Scotland, a man stood up and began quoting certain early church fathers who didn't seem to take a stand as we do on the six literal days of Creation.

I think one way to answer the question is to quote from Martin Luther, the man who started the Reformation. He said this concerning the church fathers who didn't believe in six days of creation, "Whenever we observe that the opinions of the fathers disagree with Scripture, we reverently bear with them and acknowledge them to be our elders. Nevertheless, we do not depart from authority of Scripture for their sake."

Sadly today, there's an emphasis in our churches in making man's word, not God's Word, the authority. We need to be like Martin Luther and start a new reformation in our churches to get back to the authority of the Word of God. Christians shouldn't be building their thinking upon the opinions of fallible people.

Q. *How does the account of Balaam in the Bible have anything to do with evolution?*

A. Remember the account of how the Moabite king tried to get Balaam to curse the people of Israel? God wouldn't allow this, of course. But we read later on that God judged the people of Israel and many died.

We find out that Balaam advised Balak to get some of the most beautiful women in his kingdom to draw the men of Israel into unclean and idolatrous practices. Thus, God would HAVE to judge them — which He did.

Satan uses this trick all the time. He gets God's people to compromise with the world around. I believe another example of this is the fact that so many Christians have compromised with the evolutionist teaching of millions of years. As a result of this, generations in the Church have been brought up with the idea that there's no problem with adding the world's teachings to the Bible.

This is what the doctrine of Balaam is all about. As a result, I believe God is judging His people. The increasing anti-Christian sentiment in our Western nations, and the decline of the once Christian moral-based society, is a result of God's people compromising the clear answers from God's Word.

Q. *What have you learned from your speaking tours of Scotland and England about Charles Darwin and the Church?*

A. Every time I visit Scotland and England, I'm more shocked than ever at the terrible state of the Church. These were once solidly Christian nations. There were once times of great revivals. But there's barely any vestige of biblical Christianity left in public life.

Many of the churches are now extremely liberal, and very small. What I have learned from my tours is that what has happened to England and Scotland is occurring in countries like America, and for the same reasons. The Church in America needs to wake up and learn from these once great Christian nations.

What has happened to the Church in England and Scotland is like an earthquake. What shook the Christian structure in these nations was what I call the Darwinian earthquake. The Church believed Darwin and compromised the Word of God. By rejecting Genesis as literal history, the Church itself destroyed the foundations of its own Christian doctrine.

Sadly, the Christian structure in America, which was once a Christian nation, is falling fast. And the reason? As the Church rejects the Bible in favor of evolution, the Christian structure will collapse.

Q: *Many people think Earth Day is just a time for people to remember about caring for the earth and our environment, but are there hidden motives?*

A. Of course, to the average person, the way it's portrayed in the media sounds so admirable. And it's true that we need to look after this earth that God has given man dominion over. But there's much more behind this event than just planting trees, stopping pollution, and conserving natural resources.

Christians need to understand that at the heart of Earth Day is New Age mysticism and the worship of Mother Earth (sometimes called Gaia and Sofia). In fact, Earth Day is really described in Romans 1, where Paul tells us about those who worship the creation instead of the Creator.

At many Earth Day celebrations, you'll find New Age crystals to channel through, literature on how to worship Mother Earth, and how to contact the "god" within yourself.

Most people don't realize that Earth Day is really a religious service for the New Age movement. And their teaching is based on evolutionary philosophy. They have totally rejected the true answers from the Bible. In reality, celebrating Earth Day is supporting evolution and encouraging people to worship nature.

Q. *Why are we seeing the breakdown of the family unit in our churches?*

A. First, let's see what the Bible teaches about the family. When we read Genesis, we find that the family is the FIRST and most fundamental of all human institutions that God ordained. It's obvious that the family is the backbone of the nation. If the family unit is destroyed, so goes the nation.

In Malachi, we're told that one of the primary purposes for the family, and the reason why God made Adam and Eve to be one flesh, was so that they could produce GODLY offspring.

Not just offspring, by the way, but GODLY offspring. In other words, people get married and produce children who are so trained in the Word of God, they will influence the world for Jesus Christ. Then these children will get married and themselves produce GODLY offspring to influence the world.

If you get people to doubt Genesis, which teaches the foundational beginning of the family, you undermine the family unit.

Q. *Why is it that many Christians today don't seem to be able to adequately defend the doctrines of Christianity as they once could?*

A. The major reason is because most Christians don't believe and understand the Book of Genesis.

You see, Satan has been very clever. He knows that if he can convince Christians that the Book of Genesis isn't true, then the foundations of all Christian doctrine will crumble. Ultimately, the Christian structure in the nation would collapse.

This is exactly what has happened. Christians need to wake up to the fact that the meaning of sin, marriage, clothing, death, family, and in fact all doctrines of Christianity, are dependant on the events recorded in Genesis.

For instance, what is sin? Why are all people sinners? The only way to answer these questions is to go to the Book of Genesis, where we read about the origin of sin. The first man, Adam, disobeyed God. He rebelled against his Creator. This was the original sin. Since all humans are descendants of Adam, all are sinners, and sin is rebellion against God because there was a literal rebellion, in a literal garden, by a literal man.

History as recorded in Genesis, is foundational to everything a Christian believes.

Q. *Many theologians today say that Christians can believe in evolution and millions of years of earth history. Why?*

A. The more I research this area, the more I've discovered that these theologians who compromise with Genesis are putting their trust in man's fallible theories. They're not believers in the infallible Word of God.

When you look at Bible commentaries before the 1800s, you'll find that most theologians accepted the six literal days of creation and the global flood of Noah's day. There's not a hint that they believed in a universe billions of years old.

But a change occurred in the commentaries in the past two centuries. As you read them, you notice many of the theologians writing that the days of creation were not literal days, and that the flood of Noah's day was just a local event. As you read carefully, you discover that the reason they question the creation days and the global flood is because of man's fallible theories.

Isn't it sad? These theologians take the Bible figuratively and man's theories literally!

Q. *You have said in your lectures that most Christians don't believe that God created everything in six literal days. Why?*

A. Well, the interesting thing that I've found is that the major reason most people seem to reject that God created everything in six literal days really has nothing to do with what the Bible teaches. But it has to do with outside influences.

Let me explain. I was giving a lecture at a church in England when one of the elders jumped up in the middle of my talk and actually blurted out, "But dating methods used by evolutionists PROVE that the days of Genesis can't be ordinary days."

I immediately replied, "But sir. All dating methods that evolutionists use in the present to try to go back into the past are based on all sorts of assumptions. There are many unknowns in relation to the past. You can't use man's fallible methods to give accurate dates. Anyway, 90 percent of all dating methods give dates far younger than evolutionists require."

Also, if you start with the Bible, and don't use man's unreliable methods to interpret Scripture — it's obvious that Genesis teaches ordinary days. We need to get our answers from God's Word — not man's inaccurate methods.

Q. *Why is it that so many pastors today don't seem to speak with authority anymore?*

A. I love that verse of Scripture where we're told that the people were amazed at Jesus' teaching because he spoke as one having authority, and not as the scribes.

You see, Jesus is the Word, and He spoke with the authority of the Word. Remember when He was tempted by the devil? Each time He replied, "It is written." When He was asked about marriage in Matthew 19, He said, "Have ye not read?"

Because we also have the Word of God, we can speak with the same authority. But most Christian leaders have compromised Genesis, and therefore don't really have a foundation for their doctrine. They can't preach with this same authority.

After speaking at a conference in England where I challenged the church leaders to believe in Genesis, I had many pastors come to me and admit they wanted to speak with the same boldness which they heard from me. They acknowledged that because of the influence of evolutionary ideas, they were unsure about the truths of God's Word. This included Genesis.

When Christian leaders believe in the Bible from its very first verse, they will preach with power and authority.

Q. *With so many churches around today, why do we hear of a so-called "evangelical crisis"?*

A. The answer's easy — they've lost their foundation.

Some churches feel that all they have to do is address the social needs of their people, instead of teaching them theology and what the Bible says. Other churches claim that telling people they're sinners is harmful because it gives them "a poor self-image." Some churches have shortened sermons and concentrated on dramas in order to entertain people. Other churches make political issues of everything.

And there are churches today that no longer preach from the Bible because it's "too old fashioned" and not "relevant" anymore. Other churches just preach on topics to make people feel good about themselves, not daring to say anything that might make them feel uncomfortable with their lifestyle.

All of these churches have lost sight of the importance of teaching their people what the Bible has to say about our God, our origins, sin and its consequences, and thus the real way to overcome their problems. They fail to teach the foundations that are laid down in the answer book, Genesis, that are a key to understanding the rest of the Bible.

The text of this book was adapted from "Answers . . . with Ken Ham" radio scripts. For more information on any of the topics covered in this book, please review the following resource list or contact the AiG ministry nearest you (see last page).

The Garden of Eden and the Fall

The Genesis Record – Henry Morris (Grand Rapids, MI: Baker Book House Co., 1979)

The Revised Answers Book – Don Batten, editor; Ken Ham; Jonathan Sarfati; Carl Wieland (Green Forest, AR: Master Books, Inc., 2000)

Where Did Cain Get His Wife? – Ken Ham, booklet (Answers in Genesis)

The Flood of Noah

The Revised Answers Book – Batten, editor, et al.

Noah's Ark: A Feasibility Study – John Woodmorappe (El Cajon, CA: Institute for Creation Research, 1996)

The World That Perished – John C. Whitcomb (Grand Rapids, MI: Baker Book House Co., 1988)

Amazing Bible Facts about Noah's Ark – Ken Ham and Mark Dinsmore (Groton, VT: Wellspring Books)

Raging Waters – video (Answers in Genesis)

Mount St. Helens – video (Institute for Creation Research)

Dinosaurs

The Great Dinosaur Mystery Solved – Ken Ham (Green Forest, AR: Master Books, Inc., 1998)

Dinosaurs and the Bible – Ken Ham, booklet (Answers in Genesis)

Creation Evangelism

Creation Evangelism for the New Millennium – Ken Ham (Green Forest, AR: Master Books, Inc., 1999)

Is There Really a God? – Ken Ham, booklet (Answers in Genesis)

The Gap Theory and Other Compromises

The Revised Answers Book – Batten, et al.

The Genesis Record – Morris

Unformed and Unfilled – Weston W. Fields (Collinsville, IL: Burgener Enterprises, 1976)

Evidence for Creation

Creation: Facts of Life – Gary Parker (Green Forest, AR: Master Books, Inc., 1994)

The Revised Answers Book – Batten, et al.

Stones and Bones – Carl Wieland (Green Forest, AR: Master Books, Inc., 1996)

From a Frog to a Prince — video (Answers in Genesis)

The Evolution Conspiracy — video (Jeremiah Films)

The Fossil Record

Evolution: The Fossils Still Say No! – Duane Gish (El Cajon, CA: Institute for Creation Research, 1995)

Stones and Bones – Wieland

Bone of Contention – Sylvia Baker (Green Forest, AR: Master Books, Inc., 1976)

Bones of Contention – Marvin Lubenow (Grand Rapids, MI: Baker Book House Co., 1992)

In the Image of God — video (Answers in Genesis)

Evidence for a Young Earth

The Young Earth – John Morris (Green Forest, AR: Master Books, Inc., 1994)

Mount St. Helens: Explosive Evidence — Steve Austin, video (Institute for Creation Research)

Current World Issues

The Lie: Evolution – Ken Ham (Green Forest, AR: Master Books, Inc., 1987)

The Monkey Trial — Ken Ham, video lecture (Answers in Genesis)

Genesis and the Decay of the Nations – Ken Ham (Green Forest, AR: Master Books, Inc., 1991)

The Genesis Solution — Ken Ham, video (Eden Communications)

Racism

One Blood: The Biblical Answer to Racism – Ken Ham (Green Forest, AR: Master Books, Inc., 1999)

The Revised Answers Book – Batten, et al.

Where Did the "Races" Come From? – Ken Ham, booklet (Answers in Genesis)

How you can be saved . . .

The Bible says there are five things you need to know about receiving eternal life.

1. Eternal life (heaven) is a gift. The Bible says: "The gift of God is eternal life through Jesus Christ our Lord" (Rom. 6:23). Like any other genuine gift, it is not earned or deserved. No amount of personal effort, good works, or religious deeds can earn a place in heaven. The Bible also states in Ephesians 2:8–9 that "By grace are ye saved through faith; and that not of yourselves: it is the gift of God: not of works, lest any man should boast." Why is it that no one can earn his or her way to heaven? That is because . . .

2. All humans are sinners — "For all have sinned, and come short of the glory of God" (Rom. 3:23). Sin is transgressing God's law and includes such things as lying, lusting, cheating, deceit, anger, evil thoughts, immoral behavior, and more. Because we are sinners, we cannot save ourselves. In fact, do you know how good you would have to be to save yourself by your own good deeds? Matthew 5:48 declares, "Be ye therefore perfect, even as your Father which is in heaven is perfect." Perfection is such a high standard that no one can save himself. However, in spite of our sin . . .

3. God is merciful. First John 4:8 says that "God is love" and in Jeremiah 31:3 He says, "I have loved thee with an everlasting love." Because God loves us, He doesn't want to punish us. God, however, is also just and therefore must punish sin. He says: "[I] will by no means clear the guilty" (Exod. 34:7) and "the soul that sinneth, it shall die" (Ezek. 18:4). We have a problem! Despite God's love for us, His justice demands that He must punish our sin. But there is a remedy . . .

4. Jesus Christ is the solution. The Bible tells us that Christ is the infinite God-Man. "In the beginning was the Word [Jesus]

. . . and the Word [Jesus] was God. And the Word [Jesus] was made flesh, and dwelt among us" (John 1:1–14). Jesus Christ — the last Adam — came to earth and lived a sinless life. He died on the Cross to pay the penalty for our sins and rose from the grave to purchase a place for us in heaven. "All we like sheep have gone astray; we have turned everyone to his own way; and the LORD hath laid on Him [Jesus] the iniquity of us all" (Isa. 53:6). Jesus Christ bore our sin in His body on the Cross and now offers us eternal life (heaven) as a gift (1 Pet. 2:24). How?

5. This gift is received by faith. Faith is the key that opens the door to heaven. Many people, however, mistake two things for saving faith:

a. Intellectual assent, such as believing only historical facts. However, the Bible says that even the devil believes in God (James 2:19); therefore, just believing in God is not saving faith.

b. Temporal faith, such as trusting God to solve temporary crises, including financial, family, or physical needs. While it is good to trust Christ to meet these needs, this is not saving faith.

Saving faith is trusting in Jesus Christ alone for eternal life. It means resting upon Christ alone and what He has done on the cross, rather than what you or I have done. "Believe [trust] on the Lord Jesus Christ, and thou shall be saved" (Acts 16:31).

The question that God would ask of non-believers is: Would you like to receive the gift of eternal life? You would need to transfer your trust from what you have been doing to what Christ has done for you on His cross, and then confess "with thy mouth the Lord Jesus, and shalt believe in thine heart that God hath raised Him from the dead, [and] thou shalt be saved" (Rom. 10:9).

Acts 3:19 says, "Repent ye therefore, and be converted, that your sins may be blotted out." Repentance is not only a heartfelt, sorrowful remorse for past sins, but also a change of mind, which is proven by a changed life. If you wish to repent, have your sins blotted out, and receive Christ as Savior, here is a suggested prayer:

> Oh, Jesus Christ, I know I am a sinner and do not deserve eternal life. But I believe You died to pay for my sins and rose from the grave to purchase a place in heaven for me. Lord Jesus, come into my life — take control of my life — forgive my sins and save me. I repent of my sins and now place my trust in You alone for my salvation. I desire to receive the free gift of eternal life.

If you have prayed this prayer of repentance, you have received the gift of eternal life! You are now a child of God — forever!

Just as a newborn baby grows physically, so now you need to grow spiritually. Read your Bible, at least one chapter a day. Also, spend some time talking (praying) with God.

It is also important that you regularly attend a Bible-believing church that honors Christ and teaches that the Bible is the inspired Word of God and is authoritative for every aspect of your life (2 Tim. 3:15). Seek the fellowship of Christians that can help you grow in your faith. And as you grow, tell others what Christ means to you.

If you have found new life through Christ in this book, please email us at mail@answersingenesis.org or write/call one of the Answers in Genesis ministries on the following page.

Answers in Genesis International consists of the following affiliated but independent ministries.

Answers in Genesis
P.O. Box 6330
Florence, KY 41022
USA

Answers in Genesis
P.O. Box 39005
Howick, Auckland
NEW ZEALAND

Answers in Genesis
P.O. Box 6302
Acacia Ridge DC
QLD 4110
AUSTRALIA

Answers in Genesis
P.O. Box 5262
Leicester LE2 3XU
UNITED KINGDOM

Answers in Genesis
5-420 Erb St. West
Suite 213
Waterloo, Ontario
CANADA, N2L 6K6

In addition, you may contact:

Institute for Creation Research
P.O. Box 2667
El Cajon, CA 92021
USA